Studies in Liturgical Musicology
Edited by Dr. Robin A. Leaver

1. Frans Brouwer and Robin A. Leaver (eds.). *Ars et Musica in Liturgia: Essays Presented to Casper Honders on His Seventieth Birthday*. 1994.

2. Steven Plank. *"The Way to Heavens Doore": An Introduction to Liturgical Process and Musical Style*. 1994.

3. Thomas Allen Seel. *A Theology of Music for Worship Derived from the Book of Revelation*. 1995.

4. David W. Music. *Hymnology: A Collection of Source Readings*. 1996.

5. Ulrich Meyer. *Biblical Quotation and Allusion in the Cantata Libretti of Johann Sebastian Bach*. 1997.

6. D. Dewitt Wasson. *Hymntune Index and Related Hymn Materials*. 1998.

7. David W. Music. *Instruments in Church: A Collection of Source Documents*. 1998.

Instruments in Church

A Collection of Source Documents

David W. Music

Studies in Liturgical Musicology, No. 7

The Scarecrow Press, Inc.
Lanham, Maryland, and London
1998

SCARECROW PRESS, INC.

Published in the United States of America
by Scarecrow Press, Inc.
4720 Boston Way
Lanham, Maryland 20706

4 Pleydell Gardens, Folkestone
Kent CT20 2DN, England

British Library Cataloguing in Publication Information Available

Library of Congress Cataloging-in-Publication Data

Instruments in church : a collection of source documents / [compiled and edited by] David W. Music.
p. cm. — (Studies in liturgical musicology ; no. 7)
Includes bibliographical references and index.
ISBN 0-8108-3595-9 (cloth : alk. paper)
1. Musical instruments—Religious aspects—Christianity—History—Sources. 2. Music in churches. 3. Church music. I. Music, David W., 1949- . II. Series.
ML3001.157 1999
264'.2—dc21 98-41678

The paper used in this publication meets the minimum requirements of American National Standard for Information Sciences—Permanence of Paper for Printed Library Materials, ANSI Z39.48-1984.
Manufactured in the United States of America.

To Doris, my favorite organist

Contents

Editor's Foreword

INSTRUMENTS, it seems, have always been somewhat controversial in Christian worship. From the early church to today, the issue of whether or not instruments are appropriate, valid, or necessary in worship has been constantly debated, with protagonists on both sides of the argument, as well as those who occupy the ambivalent middle ground.

There are signs in the first century that some worship songs were accompanied by instruments, for example, in the content of some of the Odes of Solomon. But by the second century, the climate had changed and unaccompanied vocal music became the norm for worship. A primary factor was the prominent use of instruments in the cultic rites of the many religions of the Greco-Roman world. Thus, by contrast, the three monotheistic religions, Judaism, Christianity, and Islam, permitted only the music of the human voice in worship. The early Church Fathers spiritualized biblical references to instruments and condemned their actual use in worship. The Byzantine liturgical tradition, along with orthodox and conservative Judaism, preserves to this day liturgical music that is entirely without the support of musical instruments.

The Catholic West shared this tradition until the flowering of polyphony in the later medieval period, when it became customary to double the vocal parts with individual instruments, a performance practice that was a primary feature of much of the liturgical music of the Renaissance. Even though the Council of Trent sought to return to the vocal ideal, in practice, instrumental sonorities were not eliminated from the music of the Roman liturgy. The Gabrielis in Venice made much use of instrumental accompaniment, and Monteverdi later extended the use of independent instrumental parts in his liturgical settings, a trend that reached its zenith in the concerted masses of Mozart and Haydn.

In the sixteenth century, the Reformed tradition followed Calvin in rejecting instrumental music in worship, though some areas, influenced by Zwingli, eliminated all music from worship. The Lutheran tradition was different, largely due to Luther's positive understanding of music. It inherited the earlier practice of instrumental doublings of voice parts, and, influenced by the Catholic practice of northern Italy, Praetorius and Schütz, among others, developed the extensive use of a wide range of instruments in their music for worship. This Lutheran tradition of instrumental liturgical music culminated in the cantatas of Bach but also overflowed into the Moravian tradition of church music, in which the use of instruments continued into the nineteenth century.

In Anglican worship there have been periods when instruments were a regular feature. The seventeenth-century Restoration anthem was customarily accompanied by strings; evangelical charity chapels made notable use of instruments in the later eighteenth century, particularly by Madan, Haweis, and Giardini at the Lock Hospital; and in the late eighteenth and early nineteenth centuries congregational singing was supported by church bands made up of strings and winds, as epitomized in Thomas Hardy's *Under the Greenwood Tree.*

By the eighteenth century, organs were normative in the churches of larger towns and cities of Europe, but in England and America they did not become widespread until the later nineteenth century. Thus, in the mid-nineteenth century, the congregation of Spurgeon's Baptist Metropolitan Tabernacle in London was singing totally without instrumental accompaniment, while some American Presbyterian congregations were using the support of a single string bass.

In the early decades of the twentieth century, controversy ensued in this country when some churches, many of them Baptist, began accompanying hymn singing with strings and brass instruments. Controversy continues as opinions differ on the admissibility and use of instruments in worship.

What David W. Music has done in this book is to draw together in chronological order some of the primary writings that deal with the issue of the use of instruments in worship. In some respects it is a sequel to his earlier book, *Hymnology: A Collection of Source Readings* (no. 4 in this series), in that it is an anthology of basic documentary source materials. It is therefore a valuable reference work that not only details the main lines of the history of the issue but also provides the necessary back-ground to the contemporary discussion of the place and purpose of instruments in worship.

Robin A. Leaver, Series Editor
Westminster Choir College of Rider University
and Drew University

Acknowledgments

APPRECIATION is expressed to the copyright owners listed below for allowing the use of copyrighted material in this book.

Hope Publishing Company for permission to print an extract taken from *Church Music and the Christian Faith* by Erik Routley, © 1978, Agape, A Division of Hope Publishing Co., Carol Stream, IL 60188. All rights reserved. Used by permission.

Leo S. Olschki for permission to quote from Claudio Sartori, *Bibliografia della Musica Strumtale Italiana stampata in Italia fino al 1700.*

Sacred Music for permission to reprint Richard J. Schuler's "Guitars and Pianos."

Peter Smith Publisher for permission to quote from William Bentley, *The Diary of Rev. William Bentley 1784-1819* (Peter Smith Publisher, Gloucester, MA, 1962).

The University of California Press for permission to quote Robert Stevenson's translation of Francisco Guerrero from *Spanish Cathedral Music in the Golden Age* (Berkeley and Los Angeles: University of California Press, 1961).

Duke University Press for permission to quote Adriano Banchieri's "Conclusioni nel suono dell' organo" from William Klenz's *Giovanni Maria Bononcini of Modena: A Chapter in Baroque Instrumental Music.* © 1962, Duke University Press. Reprinted with permission.

The Institute for Worship Studies for permission to reprint James R. Hart's articles "The Synthesizer in Worship" and "The Band in the Praise-and-Worship Tradition," from Robert E. Webber, ed., *Music and the Arts in Christian Worship*, vol. 4 of *The Complete Library of Christian Worship.*

The International Commission on English in the Liturgy for allowing reproduction of the extract from the English translation of *Documents on the Liturgy 1963-1979: Conciliar, Papal, and Curial Texts*, © 1982, International Committee on English in the Liturgy, Inc. All rights reserved.

G.I.A. Publications for permission to quote from *The Motu Proprio of Church Music of Pope Pius X: A New Translation and Commentary.* © 1950 by G.I.A. Publications, Inc., Chicago, IL. All rights reserved.

The Catholic University of America Press for permission to quote from Simon P. Wood's translation of Clement of Alexandria, *Christ the Educator*, vol. 23 of The Fathers of the Church.

E. J. Brill for permission to quote from Frank Williams's translation of *The Panarion of Epiphanius of Salamis, Book 1 (Sects 1-46).*

James W. McKinnon and Cambridge University Press for permission to quote extracts from Professor McKinnon's *Music in Early Christian Literature*.

James Andrews for permission to quote from C. Bruyn Andrews's edition of *The Torrington Diaries.*

Worship Leader magazine for permission to reprint Chuck Kraft's "Organ/Guitar Preference Reflects View of God." © 1988, CCM Communications, Nashville, TN 37205. For subscription information call 1-800-286-8099.

Oxford University Press for the use of the extract from C. H. Turner's "Niceta of Remesiana II. Introduction and Text of *De psalmodiae bono*," *Journal of Theological Studies* 24 (April 1923), 237-238.

The Choral Journal for permission to reprint Pauline Hudson's article "Can Technology Replace the Church Choir Accompanist?"

Introduction

TODAY, the use of musical instruments in the Christian church is so common as to be taken almost for granted. With a few notable exceptions, instruments are nearly ubiquitous in Christian worship services of the late twentieth century, particularly in England and America.

However, the history of the church reveals that it has had what might be called a serious love-hate affair with musical instruments. There have been periods in which groups and individuals have rejected the use of instruments of any kind, whereas others have welcomed instruments with open arms. In some cases, certain instruments have been deemed acceptable, while others were excluded for one reason or another. A decision to use musical instruments and agreement on which ones are appropriate for use in worship has not meant the end of controversy, for the persons who should play them and the music they should perform often seem to have troubled the church.

The purpose of this book is to help guide the reader through some of these issues by letting the proponents and critics of instruments speak for themselves. The volume is a collection of primary documents whose purpose is to illustrate the philosophies and uses of musical instruments throughout the history of the Christian church.

The readings have been drawn from a variety of sources, including the Bible, letters, theological treatises, chroniclers' accounts, prefaces and tables of contents of music collections, church records, ecclesiastical rulings and decrees, diaries, and periodical articles. The documents have been selected to illuminate the philosophy of the period or writer regarding the place of musical instruments in worship, as well as to illustrate the actual uses of instruments in the church. Detailed descriptions of musical instruments and playing techniques have not been included unless they demonstrate something of the philosophy or place of instrumental music in the worship service.

The contents of the book range from relatively brief selections to documents and extracts of moderate length. Whole documents or significant portions thereof have been preferred, but I have not hesitated to excise repetitious or irrelevant material. When less than a complete document or section of a document has been used, the source note that precedes the selection begins with the word *from*. Omissions within the body of a text are indicated by ellipses. Original documents or facsimiles have been used whenever possible, but where these were not available, modern editions have been readily employed.

The overall organization is chronological. The book begins with significant descriptions of the use of instruments in the Old Testament, which are not only of intrinsic interest but also form the basis for many later discussions relative to the use of instruments. Proceeding through the New Testament, the book includes the views of the early Church Fathers, the introduction of the organ into the medieval church in the West, the philosophies of the sixteenth-century continental and English reformers, and the use of instruments from the sixteenth through the twentieth centuries. Particular attention is given to documents relating to instrumental usage in England and America from the Reformation to the present.

Within each part, the chapters are arranged largely by subject matter, with similar topics being grouped together. Where possible, the chapters are themselves arranged in chronological order. It is hoped that this organization will enhance the usefulness of the book for those who desire to examine a particular approach to the use of instruments. For example, a reader who wants to compare the views of the principal sixteenth-century reformers regarding the use of instruments may simply turn to chapter 5, where he or she will find them contained in a single group.

One of my goals has been to let the original writers speak for themselves as much as possible, complete with whatever errors, misunderstandings, and harsh language they initially used. I have sought to include a balance of viewpoints where such existed, but during some eras —for example, the Church Fathers—there was considerable unanimity on the subject. For the most part, I have resisted the temptation to include parenthetical editorial remarks. Those that do appear have been inserted strictly for clarity and are easily recognizable by being placed in brackets; parenthetical remarks by other editors or translators have mostly been omitted, but where they have been retained, that fact is pointed out in the source note.

For works that were initially written in languages other than English, I have sometimes made use of translations by other persons, whose contributions are acknowledged in the source note. Where no translator's name appears in the source note, the English rendering may be assumed to be the work of the present compiler.

Regardless of the source of the translation, I have sought to clarify the specific names of musical instruments mentioned in a passage by giving the word in its original language or a transliteration either in the source note or in brackets immediately after the English rendering of the term. For example, in the passage from Clement of Alexandria that is excerpted in this volume, the source note points out that the translator has used the word *flute* as a translation of the Greek term *aulos*; more recent scholarship would suggest that *aulos* should be translated "pipe," since it was a reed instrument. In a number of translated documents, the names of the instruments have simply been transliterated into English; in these cases the original words are easily recognizable and no additional identification is necessary.

A special case is presented by the Latin word *organum*, which in ancient writings can mean not only the organ but a musical instrument of any kind (another generic Latin term for musical instruments is *instrumentum*) or a type of vocal polyphony of the late Middle Ages. *Organum* can also have nonmusical implications, referring to a tool, implement, or document (compare the modern description of a periodical as an "organ"). In some writings, the term is used in more than one sense in a single passage (e.g., Augustine). The context usually determines which meaning of *organum* was originally intended, but this is not invariably clear, and readers should keep this in mind, particularly in chapters 3 and 4.

Each writing in this volume is preceded by a note giving insight into the author and/or context of the writing, a brief commentary on significant features of the document, and full source information. In part, this prefatory note takes the place of footnotes by the present compiler. I have also generally omitted the footnotes of translators and editors whose work I have used. Thus, with one exception, the only footnotes to be found in the following pages are those of the primary writers themselves (the exception is an editor's note in the diary of Ezra Stiles that reproduces a pertinent additional writing by Stiles himself). In some cases, the footnotes were originally marginal notes. Regardless of their original form, the notes have been renumbered and set as footnotes for this book.

A few words must be said about the numbering of the psalms. In the documents themselves, these are given as found in the source. When the numbering follows the Latin Vulgate version, a Roman numeral is given in the introductory note, followed by a parenthetical reference to the Protestant numbering. Since the Vulgate and Protestant numberings differ for a good many psalms, sometimes the two numbers do not coincide. An example is the selection from Augustine's *Ennarrationes in Psalmum*, which is Psalm LVI (i.e., 56) in the Vulgate but Psalm 57 in the Protestant version.

While it should be understood that any errors to be found in the following pages are strictly my own, I readily acknowledge my indebtedness to Robert Phillips, Reference Librarian at Roberts Library, Southwestern Baptist Theological Seminary, Fort Worth, Texas, for assistance in gathering materials; Dr. Beverly Howard, Professor of Music at California Baptist College, Riverside, California, for reading a preliminary draft of the manuscript and making a number of valuable suggestions; Dr. Robin A. Leaver, editor of the Studies in Liturgical Musicology series for his encouragement to pursue this project and his timely advice; and finally to Lavon Gray, Bruce Muskrat, Vivee Peseye, Tommy Rowell, and Johnny Scheuermann, students in my Seminar in Church Music History, who used the material in an early form and helped catch a number of errors.

Abbreviations

PG J.-P. Migne, ed. *Patrologiae Cursus Completus . . . Series Graeca*. 161 vols. Paris, 1857-1887.

PL J.-P. Migne, ed. *Patrologiae Cursus Completus . . . Series Latina*. 221 vols. Garnier Fratres, 1878-1890.

WA *D. Martin Luthers Werke*. Weimar: Hermann Böhlau, 1883-1990. [*Weimar Ausgabe*]

Part I
The Bible

1
The Old Testament

THE Bible serves as the obvious beginning point for any study of the place and role of musical instruments in the church. This chapter and the one that follows incorporate most of the significant references to instruments found in the pages of the Old and New Testaments. Many of the quoted passages in these two chapters are linked directly with Hebrew or Christian worship, while others seemingly have only a peripheral relationship to religious ceremony; nevertheless, the latter references have been included for the sake of context, completeness, and because they are an integral part of the canon of scripture. Many of the passages quoted formed the basis of later arguments for or against the use of instruments. All quotations of biblical passages are taken from the King James Version. Specific verse references have been omitted from the text.

Except where otherwise noted, the English names of the instruments correspond to some form of the following Hebrew words: cymbals = *meziltayim*; pipe = *halil*; psaltery = *nebel* (pl. *nebalim*); cornet = *shofar* (pl. *shofarot*); horn = *keren*; instrument of ten strings = *ale-asor*; harp = *kinnor* (pl. *kinnorim*); minstrel = *menaggen* ("player of a stringed instrument"; pl. *nogenim*); organ = *ugab*; tabret/timbrel = *tof* (pl. *tuppim*); trumpet = *hazozerah* (pl. *hazozerot*).

The "Invention" of Musical Instruments

Genesis 4:16-22.

And Cain went out from the presence of the Lord, and dwelt in the land of Nod, on the east of Eden. And Cain knew his wife; and she conceived, and bare Enoch: and he builded a city, and called the name of the city, after the name of his son, Enoch. And unto Enoch was born Irad: and

Irad begat Mehujael: and Mehujael begat Methusael: and Methusael begat Lamech. And Lamech took unto him two wives: the name of the one was Adah, and the name of the other Zillah. And Adah bare Jabal: he was the father of such as dwell in tents, and of such as have cattle. And his brother's name was Jubal: he was the father of all such as handle the harp and organ. And Zillah, she also bare Tubal-cain, an instructer of every artificer in brass and iron: and the sister of Tubal-cain was Naamah.

Instruments Used in Prophesying
1 Samuel 9:27-10:13.

And as they were going down to the end of the city, Samuel said to Saul, Bid the servant pass on before us, (and he passed on,) but stand thou still a while, that I may shew thee the word of God. Then Samuel took a vial of oil, and poured it upon his head, and kissed him, and said, Is it not because the Lord hath anointed thee to be captain over his inheritance? When thou art departed from me to day, then thou shalt find two men by Rachel's sepulchre in the border of Benjamin at Zelzah; and they will say unto thee, The asses which thou wentest to seek are found: and, lo, thy father hath left the care of the asses, and sorroweth for you, saying, What shall I do for my son? Then shalt thou go on forward from thence, and thou shalt come to the plain of Tabor, and there shall meet thee three men going up to God to Bethel, one carrying three kids, and another carrying three loaves of bread, and another carrying a bottle of wine: And they will salute thee, and give thee two loaves of bread; which thou shalt receive of their hands. After that thou shalt come to the hill of God, where is the garrison of the Philistines: and it shall come to pass, when thou art come thither to the city, that thou shalt meet a company of prophets coming down from the high place with a psaltery, and a tabret, and a pipe, and a harp, before them; and they shall prophesy: And the Spirit of the Lord will come upon thee, and thou shalt prophesy with them, and shalt be turned into another man. And let it be, when these signs are come unto thee, that thou do as occasion serve thee; for God is with thee. And thou shalt go down before me to Gilgal; and, behold, I will come down unto thee, to offer burnt offerings, and to sacrifice sacrifices of peace offerings: seven days shalt thou tarry, till I come to thee, and shew thee what thou shalt do.

And it was so, that when he had turned his back to go from Samuel,

God gave him another heart: and all those signs came to pass that day. And when they came thither to the hill, behold, a company of prophets met him; and the Spirit of God came upon him, and he prophesied among them. And it came to pass, when all that knew him beforetime saw that, behold, he prophesied among the prophets, then the people said one to another, What is this that is come unto the son of Kish? Is Saul also among the prophets? And one of the same place answered and said, But who is their father? Therefore it became a proverb, Is Saul also among the prophets? And when he had made an end of prophesying, he came to the high place.

2 Kings 3:4-16.

And Mesha king of Moab was a sheepmaster, and rendered unto the king of Israel an hundred thousand lambs, and an hundred thousand rams, with the wool. But it came to pass, when Ahab was dead, that the king of Moab rebelled against the king of Israel.

And king Jehoram went out of Samaria the same time, and numbered all Israel. And he went and sent to Jehoshaphat the king of Judah, saying, The king of Moab hath rebelled against me: wilt thou go with me against Moab to battle? And he said, I will go up: I am as thou art, my people as thy people, and my horses as thy horses. And he said, Which way shall we go up? And he answered, The way through the wilderness of Edom. So the king of Israel went, and the king of Judah, and the king of Edom: and they fetched a compass of seven days' journey: and there was no water for the host, and for the cattle that followed them. And the king of Israel said, Alas! that the Lord hath called these three kings together, to deliver them into the hand of Moab! But Jehoshaphat said, Is there not here a prophet of the Lord, that we may enquire of the Lord by him? And one of the king of Israel's servants answered and said, Here is Elisha the son of Shaphat, which poured water on the hands of Elijah. And Jehoshaphat said, The word of the Lord is with him. So the king of Israel and Jehoshaphat and the king of Edom went down to him. And Elisha said unto the king of Israel, What have I to do with thee? get thee to the prophets of thy father, and to the prophets of thy mother. And the king of Israel said unto him, Nay: for the Lord hath called these three kings together, to deliver them into the hand of Moab. And Elisha said, As the Lord of hosts liveth, before whom I stand, surely, were it not that I regard the presence of Jehoshaphat the king of Judah, I would not look toward thee, nor see thee. But now bring me a minstrel. And it came to pass, when the minstrel played, that the hand of the Lord came upon him. And he said, Thus saith the Lord, Make this valley full of ditches.

Psalm 49:1-4.

Hear this, all ye people;
give ear, all ye inhabitants of the world:
Both low and high,
rich and poor, together.
My mouth shall speak of wisdom;
and the meditation of my heart shall be of understanding.
I will incline mine ear to a parable:
I will open my dark saying upon the harp.

The Kinnor as Therapy

1 Samuel 16:14-23, 18:6-11.

But the Spirit of the Lord departed from Saul, and an evil spirit from the Lord troubled him. And Saul's servants said unto him, Behold now, an evil spirit from God troubleth thee. Let our lord now command thy servants, which are before thee, to seek out a man, who is a cunning player on an harp: and it shall come to pass, when the evil spirit from God is upon thee, that he shall play with his hand, and thou shalt be well. And Saul said unto his servants, Provide me now a man that can play well, and bring him to me. Then answered one of the servants, and said, Behold, I have seen a son of Jesse the Bethlehemite, that is cunning in playing, and a mighty valiant man, and a man of war, and prudent in matters, and a comely person, and the Lord is with him.

Wherefore Saul sent messengers unto Jesse, and said, Send me David thy son, which is with the sheep. And Jesse took an ass laden with bread, and a bottle of wine, and a kid, and sent them by David his son unto Saul. And David came to Saul, and stood before him: and he loved him greatly; and he became his armourbearer. And Saul sent to Jesse, saying, Let David, I pray thee, stand before me; for he hath found favour in my sight. And it came to pass, when the evil spirit from God was upon Saul, that David took an harp, and played with his hand: so Saul was refreshed, and was well, and the evil spirit departed from him. . . . And it came to pass as they came, when David was returned from the slaughter of the Philistine, that the women came out of all cities of Israel, singing and dancing, to meet king Saul, with tabrets, with joy, and with instruments of musick. And the women answered one another as they played, and said, Saul hath slain his thousands, and David his ten thousands. And Saul was very wroth, and the saying displeased him; and he said, They have ascribed unto David ten thousands, and to me they have ascribed but thousands: and what can he have more but the kingdom? And Saul eyed David from that day and forward.

And it came to pass on the morrow, that the evil spirit from God came upon Saul, and he prophesied in the midst of the house: and David played with his hand, as at other times: and there was a javelin in Saul's hand. And Saul cast the javelin; for he said, I will smite David even to the wall with it. And David avoided out of his presence twice.

Instruments in the Temple Service

1 Chronicles 13:1-14. David brings the Ark of the Covenant to Jerusalem (cf. parallel passage in 2 Samuel 6:1-11).

And David consulted with the captains of thousands and hundreds, and with every leader. And David said unto all the congregation of Israel, If it seem good unto you, and that it be of the Lord our God, let us send abroad unto our brethren every where, that are left in all the land of Israel, and with them also to the priests and Levites which are in their cities and suburbs, that they may gather themselves unto us: And let us bring again the ark of our God to us: for we enquired not at it in the days of Saul. And all the congregation said that they would do so: for the thing was right in the eyes of all the people. So David gathered all Israel together, from Shihor of Egypt even unto the entering of Hemath, to bring the ark of God from Kirjath-jearim. And David went up, and all Israel, to Baalah, that is, to Kirjath-jearim, which belonged to Judah, to bring up thence the ark of God the Lord, that dwelleth between the cherubims, whose name is called on it. And they carried the ark of God in a new cart out of the house of Abinadab: and Uzza and Ahio drave the cart. And David and all Israel played before God with all their might, and with singing, and with harps, and with psalteries, and with timbrels, and with cymbals, and with trumpets.

And when they came unto the threshingfloor of Chidon, Uzza put forth his hand to hold the ark; for the oxen stumbled. And the anger of the Lord was kindled against Uzza, and he smote him, because he put his hand to the ark: and there he died before God. And David was displeased, because the Lord had made a breach upon Uzza: wherefore that place is called Perez-uzza to this day. And David was afraid of God that day, saying, How shall I bring the ark of God home to me? So David brought not the ark home to himself to the city of David, but carried it aside into the house of Obed-edom the Gittite. And the ark of the Lord remained with the family of Obed-edom in his house three months. And the Lord blessed Obed-edom, and all that he had.

1 Chronicles 15:11-28.

And David called for Zadok and Abiathar the priests, and for the Levites, for Uriel, Asaiah, and Joel, Shemaiah, and Eliel, and Amminadab, And said unto them, Ye are the chief of the fathers of the Levites: sanctify yourselves, both ye and your brethren, that ye may bring up the ark of the Lord God of Israel unto the place that I have prepared for it. For because ye did it not at the first, the Lord our God made a breach upon us, for that we sought him not after the due order. So the priests and the Levites sanctified themselves to bring up the ark of the Lord God of Israel. And the children of the Levites bare the ark of God upon their shoulders with the staves thereon, as Moses commanded according to the word of the Lord. And David spake to the chief of the Levites to appoint their brethren to be the singers with instruments of musick, psalteries and harps and cymbals, sounding, by lifting up the voice with joy. So the Levites appointed Heman the son of Joel; and of his brethren, Asaph the son of Berechiah; and of the sons of Merari their brethren, Ethan the son of Kushaiah; And with them their brethren of the second degree, Zechariah, Ben, and Jaaziel, and Shemiramoth, and Jehiel, and Unni, Eliab, and Benaiah, and Maaseiah, and Mattithiah, and Elipheleh, and Mikneiah, and Obed-edom, and Jeiel, the porters. So the singers, Heman, Asaph, and Ethan were appointed to sound with cymbals of brass; And Zechariah, and Aziel, and Shemiramoth, and Jehiel, and Unni, and Eliab, and Maaseiah, and Benaiah, with psalteries on Alamoth; And Mattithiah, and Elipheleh, and Mikneiah, and Obed-edom, and Jeiel, and Azaziah, with harps on the Sheminith to excel. And Chenaniah, chief of the Levites, was for song: he instructed about the song, because he was skilful. And Berechiah and Elkanah were doorkeepers for the ark. And Shebaniah, and Jehoshaphat, and Nethaneel, and Amasai, and Zechariah, and Benaiah, and Eliezer, the priests, did blow with the trumpets before the ark of God: and Obed-edom and Jehiah were doorkeepers for the ark.

So David, and the elders of Israel, and the captains over thousands, went to bring up the ark of the covenant of the Lord out of the house of Obed-edom with joy. And it came to pass, when God helped the Levites that bare the ark of the covenant of the Lord, that they offered seven bullocks and seven rams. And David was clothed with a robe of fine linen, and all the Levites that bare the ark, and the singers, and Chenaniah the master of the song with the singers: David also had upon him an ephod of linen. Thus all Israel brought up the ark of the covenant of the Lord with shouting, and with sound of the cornet, and with trumpets, and with cymbals, making a noise with psalteries and harps.

1 Chronicles 16:1-6. David organizes the musicians.

So they brought the ark of God, and set it in the midst of the tent that David had pitched for it: and they offered burnt sacrifices and peace offerings before God. And when David had made an end offering the burnt offerings and the peace offerings, he blessed the people in the name of the Lord. And he dealt to every one of Israel, both man and woman, to every one a loaf of bread, and a good piece of flesh, and a flagon of wine.

And he appointed certain of the Levites to minister before the ark of the Lord, and to record, and to thank and praise the Lord God of Israel: Asaph the chief, and next to him Zechariah, Jeiel, and Shemiramoth, and Jehiel, and Mattithiah, and Eliab, and Benaiah, and Obed-edom: and Jeiel with psalteries and with harps; but Asaph made a sound with cymbals; Benaiah also and Jahaziel the priests with trumpets continually before the ark of the covenant of God.

1 Chronicles 16:37-42. David organizes the musicians.

So he left there before the ark of the covenant of the Lord Asaph and his brethren, to minister before the ark continually, as every day's work required: And Obed-edom with their brethren, threescore and eight; Obed-edom also the son of Jeduthun and Hosah to be porters: And Zadok the priest, and his brethren the priests, before the tabernacle of the Lord in the high place that was at Gibeon, To offer burnt offerings unto the Lord upon the altar of the burnt offering continually morning and evening, and to do according to all that is written in the law of the Lord, which he commanded Israel; And with them Heman and Jeduthun, and the rest that were chosen, who were expressed by name, to give thanks to the Lord, because his mercy endureth for ever; And with them Heman and Jeduthun with trumpets and cymbals for those that should make a sound, and with musical instruments of God. And the sons of Jeduthun were porters.

1 Chronicles 25:1-7. David organizes the musicians.

Moreover David and the captains of the host separated to the service of the sons of Asaph, and of Heman, and of Jeduthun, who should prophesy with harps, with psalteries, and with cymbals: and the number of the workmen according to their service was: Of the sons of Asaph; Zaccur, and Joseph, and Nethaniah, and Asarelah, the sons of Asaph under the hands of Asaph, which prophesied according to the order of the king. Of Jeduthun: the sons of Jeduthun; Gedaliah, and Zeri, and Jeshaiah, Hashabiah, and Mattithiah, six, under the hands of their father Jeduthun, who prophesied with a harp, to give thanks and to praise the Lord. Of Heman: the sons of Heman; Bukkiah, Mattaniah, Uzziel, Shebuel, and Jerimoth, Hananiah, Hanani, Eliathah, Giddalti, and Romamti-ezer, Joshbekashah, Mallothi, Hothir, and Mahazioth. All these were the sons of Heman the king's seer in the words of God, to lift up the horn. And God gave to Heman fourteen sons and three daughters. All these were under the hands of their father for song in the house of the Lord, with cymbals, psalteries, and harps, for the service of the house of God, according to the king's order to Asaph, Jeduthun, and Heman. So the number of them, with their brethren that were instructed in the songs of the Lord, even all that were cunning, was two hundred fourscore and eight.

Psalm 68:24-26. The use of instruments in processions.

They have seen thy goings, O God;
  even the goings of my God, my King, in the sanctuary.
The singers went before, the players on instruments followed after;
  Among them were the damsels playing with timbrels.
Bless ye God in the congregations,
  even the Lord, from the fountain of Israel.

2 Chronicles 5:2-14. Solomon moves the ark to the Temple.

Then Solomon assembled the elders of Israel, and all the heads of the tribes, the chief of the fathers of the children of Israel, unto Jerusalem, to bring up the ark of the covenant of the Lord out of the city of David, which is Zion. Wherefore all the men of Israel assembled themselves unto the king in the feast which was in the seventh month. And all the elders of Israel came; and the Levites took up the ark. And they brought up the ark, and the tabernacle of the congregation, and all the holy vessels that were in the tabernacle, these did the priests and the Levites bring up. Also king Solomon, and all the congregation of Israel that were assembled unto him before the ark, sacrificed sheep and oxen, which could not be told nor numbered for multitude. And the priests brought in the ark of the covenant of the Lord unto his place, to the oracle of the house, into the most holy place, even under the wings of the cherubims: For the cherubims spread forth their wings over the place of the ark, and the cherubims covered the ark and the staves thereof above. And they drew out the staves of the ark, that the ends of the staves were seen from the ark before the oracle; but they were not seen without. And there it is unto this day. There was nothing in the ark save the two tablets which Moses put therein at Horeb, when the Lord made a covenant with the children of Israel, when they came out of Egypt.

And it came to pass, when the priests were come out of the holy place: (for all the priests that were present were sanctified, and did not then wait by course: Also the Levites which were the singers, all of them of Asaph, of Heman, of Jeduthun, with their sons and their brethren, being arrayed in white linen, having cymbals and psalteries and harps, stood at the east end of the altar, and with them an hundred and twenty priests sounding with trumpets:) It came even to pass, as the trumpeters and singers were as one, to make one sound to be heard in praising and thanking the Lord; and when they lifted up their voice with the trumpets and cymbals and instruments of musick, and praised the Lord, saying, For he is good; for his mercy endureth forever: that then the house was filled with a cloud, even the house of the Lord; So that the priests could not stand to minister by reason of the cloud: for the glory of the Lord had filled the house of God.

1 Kings 10:11-12. Solomon has harps and lyres constructed from almug wood.

And the navy also of Hiram, that brought gold from Ophir, brought in from Ophir great plenty of almug trees, and precious stones. And the king made of the almug trees pillars for the house of the Lord, and for the king's house, harps also and psalteries for singers: there came no such almug trees, nor were seen unto this day.

2 Chronicles 29:20-30. Hezekiah revives the Temple service.

Then Hezekiah the king rose early, and gathered the rulers of the city, and went up to the house of the Lord. And they brought seven bullocks, and seven rams, and seven lambs, and seven he goats, for a sin offering for the kingdom, and for the sanctuary, and for Judah. And he commanded the priests the sons of Aaron to offer them on the altar of the Lord. So they killed the bullocks, and the priests received the blood, and sprinkled it on the altar: likewise, when they had killed the rams, they sprinkled the blood upon the altar: they killed also the lambs, and they sprinkled the blood upon the altar. And they brought forth the he goats for the sin offering before the king and the congregation; and they laid their hands upon them: And the priests killed them, and they made reconciliation with their blood upon the altar, to make an atonement for all Israel: for the king commanded that the burnt offering and the sin offering should be made for all Israel. And he set the Levites in the house of the Lord with cymbals, with psalteries, and with harps, according to the commandment of David, and of Gad the king's seer, and Nathan the prophet: for so was the commandment of the Lord by his prophets. And the Levites stood with the instruments of David, and the priests with the trumpets. And Hezekiah commanded to offer the burnt offering upon the altar. And when the burnt offering began, the song of the Lord began also with the trumpets, and with the instruments ordained by David king of Israel. And all the congregation worshipped, and the singers sang, and the trumpeters sounded: and all this continued until the burnt offering was finished. And when they had made an end of offering, the king and all that were present with him bowed themselves, and worshipped. Moreover Hezekiah the king and the princes commanded the Levites to sing praise unto the Lord with the words of David, and of Asaph the seer. And they sang praises with gladness, and they bowed their heads and worshipped.

2 Chronicles 30:21-22. The people of Israel keep the passover at the direction of Hezekiah.

And the children of Israel that were present at Jerusalem kept the feast of unleavened bread seven days with great gladness: and the Levites and the priests praised the Lord day by day, singing with loud instruments unto the Lord. And Hezekiah spake comfortably unto all the Levites that taught the good knowledge of the Lord: and they did eat throughout the feast seven days, offering peace offerings, and making confession to the Lord God of their fathers.

Instruments in the Babylonian Exile

Psalm 137:1-4. The Hebrews silence their instruments during the Babylonian Exile.

By the rivers of Babylon,
there we sat down, yea, we wept,
when we remembered Zion.
We hanged our harps upon the willows in the midst thereof.
For there they that carried us away captive required of us a song;
And they that wasted us required of us mirth, saying,
Sing us one of the songs of Zion.
How shall we sing the Lord's song in a strange land?

Daniel 3:1-18. Nebuchadnezzar's Babylonian orchestra. In this passage, the English names of the instruments correspond to the following Aramaic words: cornet = *karna*; flute = *mashrokita*; harp = *kathros*; sackbut = *sabbeka*; psaltery = *pesanterin*; dulcimer = *sumponyah*. Recent scholarship holds that the last term does not refer to a specific musical instrument but to the playing of the entire ensemble (cf. the word *symphony*). Also, *sackbut* (a type of medieval trombone) is probably a mistranslation of *sabbeka*, which likely referred to a triangular stringed instrument.

Nebuchadnezzar the king made an image of gold, whose height was threescore cubits, and the breadth thereof six cubits: he set it up in the plain of Dura, in the province of Babylon. Then Nebuchadnezzar the king sent to gather together the princes, the governors, and the captains, the judges, the treasurers, the counsellors, the sheriffs, and all the rulers of the provinces, to come to the dedication of the image which Nebuchadnezzar the king had set up. Then the princes, the governors, and captains, the judges, the treasurers, the counsellors, the sheriffs, and all the rulers of the provinces, were gathered together unto the dedication of the image that Nebuchadnezzar the king had set up; and they stood before the image that Nebuchadnezzar had set up. Then an herald cried aloud, To you it is commanded, O people, nations, and languages, That at what time ye hear the sound of the cornet, flute, harp, sackbut, psaltery, dulcimer, and all kinds of musick, ye fall down and worship the golden image that Nebuchadnezzar the king hath set up: And whoso falleth not down and worshippeth shall the same hour be cast into the midst of a burning fiery furnace. Therefore at that time, when all the people heard the sound of the cornet, flute, harp, sackbut, psaltery, and all kinds of musick, all the people, the nations, and the languages, fell down and worshipped the golden image that Nebuchadnezzar the king had set up.

Wherefore at that time certain Chaldeans came near, and accused the Jews. They spake and said to the king Nebuchadnezzar, O king, live for ever. Thou, O king, hast made a decree, that every man that shall hear the sound of the cornet, flute, harp, sackbut, psaltery, and dulcimer, and all kinds of musick, shall fall down and worship the golden image: And whoso falleth not down and worshippeth, that he should be cast into the midst of a burning fiery furnace. There are certain Jews whom thou hast set over the affairs of the province of Babylon, Shadrach, Meshach, and Abednego; these men, O king, have not regarded thee: they serve not thy gods, nor worship the golden image which thou hast set up.

Then Nebuchadnezzar in his rage and fury commanded to bring Shadrach, Meshach, and Abednego. Then they brought these men before the king. Nebuchadnezzar spake and said unto them, Is it true, O Shadrach, Meshach, and Abednego, do not ye serve my gods, nor worship the golden image which I have set up? Now if ye be ready that at what time ye hear the sound of the cornet, flute, harp, sackbut, psaltery, dulcimer, and all kinds of musick, ye fall down and worship the image which I have made; well: but if ye worship not, ye shall be cast the same hour into the midst of a burning fiery furnace; and who is that God that shall deliver you out of my hands? Shadrach, Meshach, and Abednego, answered and said to the king, O Nebuchadnezzar, we are not careful to answer thee in this matter. If it be so, our God whom we serve is able to deliver us from the burning fiery furnace, and he will deliver us out of thine hand, O king. But if not, be it known unto thee, O king, that we will not serve thy gods, nor worship the golden image which thou hast set up.

Instruments in the Second Temple

Ezra 3:10-11. After the Babylonian Exile the Temple foundation is relaid under the direction of Ezra.

And when the builders laid the foundation of the temple of the Lord, they set the priests in their apparel with trumpets, and the Levites the sons of Asaph with cymbals, to praise the Lord, after the ordinance of David king of Israel. And they sang together by course in praising and giving thanks unto the Lord; because he is good, for his mercy endureth for ever toward Israel. And all the people shouted with a great shout, when they praised the Lord, because the foundation of the house of the Lord was laid.

Nehemiah 12:27-43. Nehemiah's rededication of the walls of Jerusalem.

And at the dedication of the wall of Jerusalem they sought the Levites out of all their places, to bring them to Jerusalem, to keep the dedication with gladness, both with thanksgivings, and with singing, with cymbals, psalteries, and with harps. And the sons of the singers gathered themselves together, both out of the plain country round about Jerusalem, and from the villages of Netophathi; Also from the house of Gilgal, and out of the fields of Geba and Azmaveth: for the singers had builded them villages round about Jerusalem. And the priests and the Levites purified themselves, and purified the people, and the gates, and the wall. Then I brought up the princes of Judah upon the wall, and appointed two great companies of them that gave thanks, whereof one went on the right hand upon the wall toward the dung gate: And after them went Hoshaiah, and half of the princes of Judah, And Azariah, Ezra, and Meshullam, Judah, and Benjamin, and Shemaiah, and Jeremiah, And certain of the priests' sons with trumpets; namely, Zechariah the son of Jonathan, the son of Shemaiah, the son of Mattaniah, the son of Michaiah, the son of Zaccur, the son of Asaph: And his brethren, Shemaiah, and Azarael, Milalai, Gilalai, Maai, Nethaneel, and Judah, Hanani, with the musical instruments of David the man of God, and Ezra the scribe before them. And at the fountain gate, which was over against them, they went up by the stairs of the city of David, at the going up of the wall, above the house of David, even unto the water gate eastward. And the other company of them that gave thanks went over against them, and I after them, and the half of the people upon the wall, from beyond the tower of the furnaces even unto the broad wall; And from above the gate of Ephraim, and above the old gate, and above the fish gate and the tower of Hananeel, and the tower of Meah, even unto the sheep gate: and they stood still in the prison gate. So stood the two companies of them that gave thanks in the house of God, and I, and the half of the rulers with me: And the priests; Eliakim, Maaseiah, Miniamin, Michaiah, Elioenai, Zechariah, and Hananiah, with trumpets; And Maaseiah, and Shemaiah, and Eleazar, and Uzzi, and Jehohanan, and Malchijah, and Elam, and Ezer. And the singers sang loud, with Jezrahiah their overseer. Also that day they offered great sacrifices, and rejoiced: for God had made them rejoice with great joy: the wives also and the children rejoiced: so that the joy of Jerusalem was heard even afar off.

The Psalms Command the Playing of Instruments

Psalm 33:1-3.

Rejoice in the Lord, O ye righteous:
for praise is comely for the upright.
Praise the Lord with harp:
sing unto him with the psaltery and an instrument of ten strings.
Sing unto him a new song;
play skilfully with a loud noise.

Psalm 81:1-4.

Sing aloud unto God our strength:
make a joyful noise unto the God of Jacob.
Take a psalm, and bring hither the timbrel,
the pleasant harp with the psaltery.
Blow up the trumpet [*shofar*] in the new moon,
in the time appointed, on our solemn feast day.
For this was a statute for Israel,
and a law of the God of Jacob.

Psalm 92:1-4.

It is a good thing to give thanks unto the Lord,
and to sing praises unto thy name, O most High:
To shew forth thy lovingkindness in the morning,
and thy faithfulness every night,
Upon an instrument of ten strings, and upon the psaltery;
upon the harp with a solemn sound.
For thou, Lord, hast made me glad through thy work:
I will triumph in the works of thy hands.

Psalm 144:9.

I will sing a new song unto thee, O God:
upon a psaltery and an instrument of ten strings will I sing praises unto thee.

Psalm 150.

Praise ye the Lord.
Praise God in his sanctuary:
praise him in the firmament of his power.
Praise him for his mighty acts:
praise him according to his excellent greatness.
Praise him with the sound of the trumpet [*shofar*]:
praise him with the psaltery and harp.
Praise him with the timbrel and dance:
praise him with stringed instruments and organs.
Praise him upon the loud cymbals [*zilzele*]:
praise him upon the high sounding cymbals [*zilzele*].
Let every thing that hath breath praise the Lord.
Praise ye the Lord.

Prophetic Denunciations of Instruments

Isaiah 5:11-13.

Woe unto them that rise up early in the morning, that they may follow strong drink; that continue until night, till wine inflame them! And the harp, and the viol [*nebel*], the tabret, and pipe, and wine, are in their feasts: but they regard not the work of the Lord, neither consider the operation of his hands.

Therefore my people are gone into captivity, because they have no knowledge: and their honourable men are famished, and their multitude dried up with thirst.

Amos 5:21-24.

I hate, I despise your feast days, and I will not smell in your solemn assemblies. Though ye offer me burnt offerings and your meat offerings, I will not accept them: neither will I regard the peace offerings of your fat beasts. Take thou away from me the noise of thy songs; for I will not hear the melody of thy viols [*nebalim*]. But let judgment run down as waters, and righteousness as a mighty stream.

Amos 6:1, 4-7.

Woe to them that are at ease in Zion, and trust in the mountain of Samaria, which are named chief of the nations, to whom the house of Israel came! . . . That lie upon beds of ivory, and stretch themselves upon their couches, and eat the lambs out of the flock, and the calves out of the midst of the stall; That chant to the sound of the viol [*nebel*], and invent to themselves instruments of musick, like David; That drink wine in bowls, and anoint themselves with the chief ointments: but they are not grieved for the affliction of Joseph.

Therefore now shall they go captive with the first that go captive, and the banquet of them that stretched themselves shall be removed.

2
The New Testament

THIS chapter includes the most important references to instruments from the New Testament. The passages are all quoted from the King James Version. Specific verse references have been omitted from the text. Except where otherwise noted, the English names of the instruments correspond to some form of the following Greek words: cymbal = *kumbalon*; pipe = *aulos*; harp = *kithara*; trumpet = *salpinx*; minstrels = *aulos* players.

The *Aulos* Used at Funerals and by Children at Play

Matthew 9:18-19, 23-25.

While he spake these things unto them, behold, there came a certain ruler, and worshipped him, saying, My daughter is even now dead: but come and lay thy hand upon her, and she shall live. And Jesus arose, and followed him, and so did his disciples. . . . And when Jesus came into the ruler's house, and saw the minstrels and the people making a noise, He said unto them, Give place: for the maid is not dead, but sleepeth. And they laughed him to scorn. But when the people were put forth, he went in, and took her by the hand, and the maid arose.

Matthew 11:16-17. Jesus compares his generation to children playing the *aulos*.

But whereunto shall I liken this generation? It is like unto children sitting in the markets, and calling unto their fellows, And saying, We have piped unto you, and ye have not danced; we have mourned unto you, and ye have not lamented.

Paul's Metaphorical Use of Instruments

1 Corinthians 13:1-3. "Sounding brass" may refer to metal reflectors placed in Greek theaters to amplify the sound rather than to a musical instrument.

Though I speak with the tongues of men and of angels, and have not charity, I am become as sounding brass [*chalkos echon*], or a tinkling cymbal. And though I have the gift of prophecy, and understand all mysteries, and all knowledge; and though I have all faith, so that I could remove mountains, and have not charity, I am nothing. And though I bestow all my goods to feed the poor, and though I give my body to be burned, and have not charity, it profiteth me nothing.

1 Corinthians 14:6-19. Several later writers used this passage as a key argument against the use of instruments in the church. In addition to the obvious references to instruments, these authors drew a parallel between the fact that instruments cannot produce intelligible words and the "unknown tongues" of the Pauline epistle.

Now, brethren, if I come unto you speaking with tongues, what shall I profit you, except I shall speak to you either by revelation, or by knowledge, or by prophesying, or by doctrine? And even things without life giving sound, whether pipe or harp, except they give a distinction in the sounds, how shall it be known what is piped or harped? For if the trumpet give an uncertain sound, who shall prepare himself to the battle? So likewise ye, except ye utter by the tongue words easy to be understood, how shall it be known what is being spoken? for ye shall speak into the air. There are, it may be, so many kinds of voices in the world, and none of them is without signification. Therefore if I know not the meaning of the voice, I shall be unto him that speaketh a barbarian, and he that speaketh shall be a barbarian unto me. Even so ye, forasmuch as ye are zealous of spiritual gifts, seek that ye may excel to the edifying of the church. Wherefore let him that speaketh in an unknown tongue pray that he may interpret. For if I pray in an unknown tongue, my spirit prayeth, but my understanding is unfruitful. What is it then? I will pray with the spirit, and I will pray with the understanding also: I will sing with the spirit, and I will sing with the understanding also. Else when thou shalt bless with the spirit, how shall he that occupieth the room of the unlearned say Amen at thy giving of thanks, seeing he understandeth not what thou sayest? For thou verily giveth thanks well, but the other is not edified. I thank my God, I speak with tongues more than ye all: Yet in the church I had rather speak five words with my understanding, that by my voice I might teach others also, than ten thousand words in an unknown tongue.

The "Last Trumpet"

1 Corinthians 15:50-52.

Now this I say, brethren, that flesh and blood cannot inherit the kingdom of God; neither doth corruption inherit incorruption. Behold, I shew you a mystery; We shall not all sleep, but we shall all be changed, In a moment, in the twinkling of an eye, at the last trump: for the trumpet shall sound, and the dead shall be raised incorruptible, and we shall be changed.

1 Thessalonians 4:13-18.

But I would not have you to be ignorant, brethren, concerning them which are asleep, that ye sorrow not, even as others which have no hope. For if we believe that Jesus died and rose again, even so them also which sleep in Jesus will God bring with him. For this we say unto you by the word of the Lord, that we which are alive and remain unto the coming of the Lord shall not prevent them which are asleep. For the Lord himself shall descend from heaven with a shout, with the voice of the archangel, and with the trump of God: and the dead in Christ shall rise first: Then we which are alive and remain shall be caught up together with them in the clouds, to meet the Lord in the air: and so shall we ever be with the Lord. Wherefore comfort one another with these words.

Revelation 8:1-2, 6-7; 11:15.

And when he had opened the seventh seal, there was silence in heaven about the space of half an hour. And I saw the seven angels which stood before God; and to them were given seven trumpets. . . . And the seven angels which had the seven trumpets prepared themselves to sound. The first angel sounded, . . . And the seventh angel sounded; and there were great voices in heaven, saying, The kingdoms of this world are become the kingdoms of our Lord, and of his Christ; and he shall reign for ever and ever.

Instruments Are Silenced in the Coming Destruction of "Babylon"
Revelation 18:21-24.

And a mighty angel took up a stone like a great millstone, and cast it into the sea, saying, Thus with violence shall that great city Babylon be thrown down, and shall be found no more at all. And the voice of harpers, and musicians, and of pipers, and trumpeters, shall be heard no more at all in thee; and no craftsman, of whatsoever craft he be, shall be found any more in thee; and the sound of a millstone shall be heard no more at all in thee; And the light of a candle shall shine no more at all in thee; and the voice of the bridegroom and of the bride shall be heard no more at all in thee: for thy merchants were the great men of the earth; for by thy sorceries were all nations deceived. And in her was found the blood of prophets, and of saints, and of all that were slain upon the earth.

Instruments in Heavenly Worship
Revelation 5:6-10.

And I beheld, and, lo, in the midst of the throne and of the four beasts, and in the midst of the elders, stood a Lamb as it had been slain, having seven horns and seven eyes, which are the seven Spirits of God sent forth into all the earth. And he came and took the book out of the right hand of him that sat upon the throne. And when he had taken the book, the four beasts and four and twenty elders fell down before the Lamb, having every one of them harps, and golden vials full of odours, which are the prayers of the saints. And they sung a new song, saying, Thou art worthy to take the book, and to open the seals thereof: for thou wast slain, and hast redeemed us to God by thy blood out of every kindred, and tongue, and people, and nation; And hast made us unto our God kings and priests: and we shall reign on the earth.

Revelation 14:1-3.

And I looked, and, lo, a Lamb, stood on the mount Sion, and with him an hundred forty and four thousand, having his Father's name written in their foreheads. And I heard a voice from heaven, as the voice of many waters, and as the voice of a great thunder: and I heard the voice of harpers harping on their harps: And they sung as it were a new song before the throne, and before the four beasts, and the elders: and no man could learn that song but the hundred and forty and four thousand, which were redeemed from the earth.

Revelation 15:1-4.

And I saw another sign in heaven, great and marvellous, seven angels having the seven last plagues; for in them is filled up the wrath of God. And I saw as it were a sea of glass mingled with fire: and them that had gotten the victory over the beast, and over his image, and over his mark, and over the number of his name, stand on the sea of glass, having the harps of God. And they sing the song of Moses the servant of God, and the song of the Lamb, saying, Great and marvellous are thy works, Lord God Almighty; just and true are thy ways, thou King of saints. Who shall not fear thee, O Lord, and glorify thy name? for thou only art holy: for all nations shall come and worship before thee; for thy judgments are made manifest.

Part II
The Postbiblical and Medieval Eras

3
The Church Fathers Reject Instrumental Music

THE centuries immediately following the close of the New Testament are often called the "patristic period" after the Church Fathers, a group of (mostly) Greek and Latin writers who laid the liturgical and theological foundations for the subsequent development of the faith. Much of the work of the Fathers was concentrated on defending the new religion against its pagan critics, formulating and defending orthodox doctrine, and providing forms of worship; thus, it is not surprising that they seldom addressed music directly.

However, there are many passing references to music scattered throughout the writings of the Fathers. Most of the passages deal with psalmody and vocal music, but a few are concerned with musical instruments. The authors of these passages were almost unanimous in rejecting the use of instruments. The Fathers brought three basic arguments to bear on the question of instruments: (1) instruments and other "ceremonies" were characteristic of the "infancy" of the church (i.e., the Jewish Dispensation), while the church was now in its maturity (the Christian Dispensation); thus, (2) the numerous references to instruments and instrumental music in the Old Testament should be interpreted symbolically; and (3) instruments were associated with immoral practices, as even some pagan writers had noted. This last reason was the most compelling, since the objections of the Fathers to instruments seem to have been based largely upon moral, rather than theological or liturgical, grounds. As will be observed from the writings given in this chapter, the Fathers do not seem to have been writing in reaction to contemporary Christian practice. That is, they were not trying to correct abuses that had crept into the Christian church, for there is very little evidence that instruments ever formed a part of Christian worship during its practice in the early centuries. Instead, the early Christian writers opposed musical instruments in any area of life; to be a player of a musical instrument was equated with being an immoral person, regardless of where the instrument was played or what music was performed. Perhaps other reasons for not using instruments were operative as well, such as the fact that during periods of persecution, noisy instruments would give away Christian meeting places, but this does not seem to have ever been mentioned by the Fathers themselves.

Apart from their intrinsic interest, the writings of the Fathers that deal with instrumental music are significant because they have formed the basis for many later arguments against instruments, particularly during the Reformation. The excerpts that follow have been grouped according to the three basic arguments of the Fathers regarding instruments. Within each grouping, the writings are organized chronologically by the author's date of death. In a few cases, a passage deals with more than one argument; in such instances, the writing is categorized according to the dominant approach to the subject.

Ignatius of Antioch

Little is known about the life of Ignatius of Antioch (d. ca. 110) except that he served as the third bishop of Antioch and was martyred in the Colosseum at Rome during the reign of Emperor Trajan. Seven letters, all apparently written as Ignatius was being carried to Rome for his martyrdom, have been generally accepted as authentic. One of these was addressed to Polycarp; the remainder were written to Christian communities in Ephesus, Magnesia, Tralles, Rome, Philadelphia, and Smyrna. In the course of the letter to the Ephesians, Ignatius compares the unity of bishop and presbyters to the well-tuned strings of a *cithara*, while in that to the Philadelphians he uses the *cithara* as a symbol of the bishop's fidelity to God's commandments. These passages are among the earliest examples of allegorical interpretation of a musical instrument by one of the Church Fathers, an approach that was to become important to later Christian writers in explaining (or explaining away) the presence of instruments in the Old and New Testaments.

Ignatius of Antioch, Letter to the Ephesians, IV. *PG* V, 648. Translated in Alexander Roberts and James Donaldson, eds., *The Ante-Nicene Fathers*, American ed., ed. A. Cleveland Coxe (New York: Charles Scribner's Sons, 1905), I, 50-51. In both of the following extracts, the word *harp* is used as a translation of the Greek *cithara*.

Wherefore it is fitting that ye should run together in accordance with the will of your bishop, which thing also ye do. For your justly renowned presbytery, worthy of God, is fitted as exactly to the bishop as the strings are to the harp. Therefore in your concord and harmonious love, Jesus Christ is sung. And do ye, man by man, become a choir, that being harmonious in love, and taking up the song of God in unison, ye may with one voice sing to the Father through Jesus Christ, so that He may both hear you, and perceive by your works that ye are indeed the members of His Son. It is profitable, therefore, that you should live in an unblameable unity, that thus ye may always enjoy communion with God.

Ignatius of Antioch, Letter to the Philadelphians, I. *PG* V, 697. Translated in Roberts and Donaldson, *Ante-Nicene Fathers*, 79. The brackets around the words *weal* and *of God* are those of the original translator.

Which bishop, I know, obtained the ministry which pertains to the common [weal], not of himself, neither by men, nor through vainglory, but by the love of God the Father, and the Lord Jesus Christ; at whose meekness I am struck with admiration, and who by his silence is able to accomplish more than those who vainly talk. For he is in harmony with the commandments [of God], even as the harp is with its strings. Wherefore my soul declares his mind towards God a happy one, knowing it to be virtuous and perfect, and that his stability as well as freedom from all anger is after the example of the infinite meekness of the living God.

Evagrius Ponticus

Once attributed to Origen (ca. 185-ca. 254), the pupil of Clement of Alexandria and his successor as head of the Alexandrian Catechetical School, the work quoted below is now thought to have been largely the work of Evagrius Ponticus (346-399). Though counted among orthodox theologians during his lifetime, after his death Evagrius was suspected of heresy, and his teachings were eventually condemned by the second Council of Constantinople (553).

Evagrius of Pontus, *Selecta in psalmos*, XXXII, 2-3. *PG* XII, 1304. Translated by James McKinnon in *Music in Early Christian Literature* (Cambridge: Cambridge University Press, 1987), 38-39.

'Praise the Lord on the cithara, sing to him on the psaltery of ten strings, etc.' The cithara is the practical soul set in motion by the commandments of God; the psaltery is the pure mind set in motion by spiritual knowledge. The musical instruments of the Old Testament are not unsuitable for us if understood spiritually: figuratively the body can be called a cithara and the soul a psaltery, which are likened musically to the wise man who fittingly employs the limbs of the body and the powers of the soul as strings. Sweetly sings he who sings in the mind, uttering spiritual songs, singing in his heart to God. The ten strings stands for ten sinews, for a string is a sinew. And the body can also be said to be the psaltery of ten strings, as it has five senses and five powers of the soul, with each power arising from a respective sense.

> Evagrius of Pontus, *Selecta in psalmos*, CL, 3-5. *PG* XII, 1684-1685. Translated by McKinnon in *Music in Early Christian Literature*, 39. The parenthetical Greek phrase in the third paragraph is given as found in McKinnon.

'Praise him in the sound of the trumpet, etc.' According to the spiritual meaning of what is said in Numbers on the construction of the trumpet, it is made so that in its sound we might praise God. These very trumpets, I would say, are indicated in this passage: 'For the trumpet will sound and the dead rise incorruptible' (I Cor 15.52); and in this: 'In the voice of the archangel and in the trumpet of God, he will come down from heaven' (I Thess 4.16). Then there is the feast of the new moon of the seventh month commemorated by trumpets; as it is written: 'Sound the trumpet at the new moon—on the well-omened day of our feast' (Ps. 80.3).

Concerning the same. The trumpet is the contemplative mind, the mind which has accepted spiritual teaching.

'Praise him on the psaltery and cithara, praise him on the tympanum and in the dance, praise him with strings and the instrument (Χορδαῖς χαὶ ὀργάνῳ), praise him on the well sounding cymbals, praise him on the clangorous cymbals, etc.' The cithara is the practical soul activated by the commandments of Christ. The tympanum is the death of covetousness through goodness itself; the dance the symphony of rational souls speaking in unison and avoiding dissension. The strings are the harmony of the balanced sound of virtues and instruments. The instrument is the church of God, made up of contemplative and active souls. The well sounding cymbal is the active soul, fixed upon the desire for Christ; the clangorous cymbal is the pure mind made live by the salvation of Christ.

Concerning the same. The many strings brought together in harmony, each ordered musically in its proper place, are the many commandments and the doctrines concerning many things, which exhibit no discord among themselves. The instrument embracing all this is the soul of the man wise in Christ.

Concerning the same. He who speaks with the tongues of men and of angels, but does not have charity, is not a well sounding cymbal.

Augustine of Hippo

Augustine of Hippo (354–430) is probably the best known of the early Christian writers. Converted to Christianity under the influence of Ambrose, Bishop of Milan, Augustine became Bishop of Hippo in 395. Augustine's most widely read work is *De civitate Dei* (The City of God). In his commentary on Psalm LVI (57), he gives a typical allegorical interpretation of the psaltery and cithara. In the original Latin version of this passage, Augustine used two generic terms for musical instruments, *instrumentum* and *organum*. The latter is, of course, also the root of the word *organ*, and in his commentary the author uses the term in both meanings. The organ that is referred to is the *hydraulis*, which at the time was a strictly secular instrument and formed no part of Christian worship. In the following passage, the words *instrumentum* and *organum* have been transliterated into English to clarify their usage. The reader should remember that, except for the obvious reference to the organ that is "inflated by a bellows," the "organs" referred to below simply refer to instruments in general.

Augustine, *Enarrationes in Psalmum*, Ps. LVI (57), 16. *PL* XXXVI, 671.

"Arise, my glory." That which fled from the face of Saul in the cave, "Arise, my glory," Jesus may be glorified after the passion. "Awake, psaltery and cithara." By what is it called, how does it arise? I see two organs, but one body of Christ: one flesh has risen again, so two organs have risen. In other words, one organ is the psaltery, the other the cithara. Organs refer to all instruments of music, not just to the large instrument inflated by a bellows; but whatever is suitable for making sound, and is physical, which uses an instrument that may be sounded, is called an organ. However, these organs have been distinguished from one another; I want to show, as much as the Lord allows, both how they have been distinguished and by what means, and how it might be said of both, "Arise." Now we have said that one flesh of the Lord has been raised again; and it says, "Arise, psaltery and cithara." The psaltery is an organ that produces sound by striking with the hands and has strings that can be stretched; but the place from which the strings resonate, the hollow wood that hangs down and resounds by making the air vibrate, is in the upper part. The cithara has the same type of hollow wood but resonates from the lower part. Therefore, in the psaltery the strings resonate from above; in the cithara, however, the strings resonate from below; this is the difference between the psaltery and the cithara. What then do these two instruments signify to us? For Christ our Lord God stirs up his psaltery and his cithara, saying, "I will rise up early." I reflect upon this because you already acknowledge the Lord's resurrection. We read in the Gospel: Behold the hour of resurrection. How long was Christ looked for in the shadows? I know that this is perplexing; he was resurrected early (Mark 16:2). But what is the psaltery? What is the cithara? Through his own flesh the Lord worked two kinds of actions, miracles and sufferings: the miracles were from above, the sufferings from below. Indeed, those miracles that were done were divine, but they were done through the body and the flesh. Thus, the flesh working the divine is the psaltery: the unyielding flesh of humanity is the cithara. The psaltery will sound; the blind will see, the deaf hear, the paralytics move, the lame walk, the sick rise up, the dead be raised; this is the sound of the psaltery. The cithara will also sound; one may hunger, thirst, sleep, be bound, scourged, ridiculed, crucified, buried. Therefore, when you see that something has resonated in the flesh from both above and below, one flesh has risen again, and in one flesh we also understand the psaltery and cithara. For those two kinds of actions have fulfilled the Gospel, and it is being preached among the nations; thus the miracles and sufferings of the Lord may be proclaimed.

Eusebius of Caesarea

Eusebius of Caesarea (ca. 260-ca. 339) was born in Palestine and studied under Pamphilus of Caesarea. He left Caesarea to escape the persecution of Christians by the Roman emperor Diocletian, settling first in Tyre, then in Egypt. In about 313, Eusebius became bishop of Caesarea. He attended the Council of Nicaea in 325, and the creed he wrote for Caesarea became a model for the subsequent Nicene Creed, the first official confession of faith of the Christian church. Eusebius is best known as the author of the earliest history of the church, which he carried down to 324, but he wrote many other works as well, including a commentary on the psalms, from which the following extract is taken. In this commentary, Eusebius became one of the first to suggest that the use of musical instruments allowed under the "old covenant" was to be abolished under the "new."

Eusebius of Caesarea, *In psalmum*, XCI, 4. *PG* XXIII, 1172-1173. Translated by McKinnon in *Music in Early Christian Literature*, 97-98. The parenthetical Greek phrase in the last sentence is given as found in McKinnon.

When formerly the people of the circumcision worshipped through symbols and types, it was not unreasonable that they raised hymns to God on psalteries and cithara, and that they did this on the days of the Sabbath, thus clearly violating the required rest and transgressing the law of the Sabbath. We, however, maintain the Jewish law inwardly, according to the saying of the Apostle: 'For he is not a real Jew who is one outwardly, nor is real circumcision something external and physical, but he is a Jew who is one inwardly, and real circumcision is a matter of the heart, spiritual and not literal' (Rom 2.28-9); and it is upon a living psaltery and an animate cithara and in spiritual songs that we render the hymn. And so more sweetly pleasing to God than any musical instrument would be the symphony of the people of God, by which, in every church of God, with kindred spirit and single disposition, with one mind and unanimity of faith and piety, we raise melody in unison (ὁμόφωνον μέλος) in our psalmody.

Niceta of Remesiana

Niceta of Remesiana (d. ca. 414) became bishop of Remesiana (present-day Bela Palanka in the former Yugoslavia) about 366. Largely forgotten by later ages, many of his works were attributed to other writers, including the similarly named Nicetius of Trier, until the twentieth century. He may have been the author of the *Te Deum Laudamus*. In common with many of the other Church Fathers, Niceta observed that the instruments used in Old Testament worship were a part of the "old law" and were now to be interpreted symbolically as parts of the body.

From Niceta of Remesiana, *De utilitate hymnorum*, XI. C. H. Turner, "Niceta of Remesiana II. Introduction and Text of *De psalmodiae bono*," *Journal of Theological Studies* 24 (April 1923), 237-238. In the following translation, the English names of the instruments correspond to some form of the following Latin words: trumpet = *tuba*; harp = *cythara*; cymbals = *cymbala*; drum = *tympanum*.

Beloved, it would take too long if I spoke in detail of what is contained in the history of the psalms, particularly given the fact that something ought to be presented from the New Testament in confirmation of the Old, not that it may be thought an inhibition of the service of psalmody, such as the observance of much of the old law which has been discontinued. For what is fleshly is rejected, including circumcision, the sabbath, sacrifices, discrimination in foods, trumpets, harps, cymbals, drums: which now are all understood to resonate better in the members of the human being. Daily baptisms, observance of new moons, and painstaking inspection for leprosy have entirely ceased and been abrogated, even if these were necessary for a time because of their childishness. On the other hand, spiritual things—among which are faith, piety, prayer, fasting, patience, chastity, and praise—have been increased, not lessened.

Theodoret of Cyrrhus

Theodoret of Cyrrhus (ca. 393-ca. 458) was born and studied in Antioch of Syria, becoming bishop of Cyrrhus, a small town near his birthplace, in 423. In 431 the Council of Ephesus condemned his friend and onetime fellow student Nestorius (d. ca. 440) for heresy because of his belief that Jesus was both fully human and fully divine. While Theodoret was not in full agreement with Nestorius, he opposed attempts to persecute his colleague, for which he was roundly criticized and ultimately deposed at another council in Ephesus in 449. Nestorius's views were ultimately vindicated at the Council of Chalcedon, and Theodoret was restored to his see. Theodoret's most famous writing was his continuation of Eusebius's history of the church. In his *Quaestiones et responsiones*, Theodoret added his voice to those who considered instruments to be a part of the "childhood" of the church.

Theodoret of Cyrus, *Quaestiones et responsiones ad orthodoxos*, CVII. *PG* VI, 1353. Translated by McKinnon in *Music in Early Christian Literature*, 107. The parenthetical Greek phrase in the response is given as found in McKinnon.

Question 107 If songs were invented by unbelievers as a ruse, and introduced to those under the Law because of their simple mindedness, while those under Grace have adopted better practices, unlike those customs just mentioned, why have they used these songs in the churches as did the children of the Law?

Response It is not singing as such which befits the childish, but singing with lifeless instruments, and with dancing and finger clappers (χροτάλων); wherefore the use of such instruments and other things appropriate to those who are childish is dispensed with in the churches and singing alone has been left over.

Clement of Alexandria

Clement of Alexandria (Titus Flavius Clemens, 150-ca. between 211 and 215), the son of pagan parents, was probably a native of Athens. His conversion to Christianity may have come about through the influence of Pantaenus, the head of the famous catechetical school at Alexandria, Egypt. In about A.D. 190, Clement succeeded Pantaenus as director of the school, where he became the teacher of another significant early Greek church father, Origen. Clement's best-known writing, *Paedagogus* (The Instructor), was written about 200. In this work he summarizes for his readers the behavior to be exhibited by Christians, especially in the liturgy and at the Eucharistic feast. One passage in his description implies that some early Christians might have sung psalms to the accompaniment of the *cithara* or *lyra*. However, the surrounding sections associate musical instruments with pagan revelry and supposed power over nature. Like so many of the Church Fathers, Clement suggests that physical musical instruments are of little use to the Christian, since—metaphorically speaking—the Christian's whole body is to be an instrument in praise of Christ.

Clement of Alexandria, *Paedagogus*, Book 2, Chapter 4. Source: *PG* VIII, 439-446. Translated by Simon P. Wood in Clement of Alexandria, *Christ the Educator*, vol. 23 of The Fathers of the Church (New York: Fathers of the Church, 1954), 129-133. Except where otherwise noted, the English names for the instruments in this passage correspond to some form of the following Greek words: bugle = *cerati* (an animal horn), castanets = *crotalon*, cymbal = *cymbalon*, drum = *tympanon*, flute = *aulos*, harp = *psalterion*, horn = *syrinx*, lyre = *lyra*, organ = *organo*, trumpet = *salpinx*, timbal = *tympanon*. The word *pectisin* undoubtedly refers to the *pektis*, a two-stringed instrument (not a flute, as given below).

In the feasts of reason that we have, let the wild celebrations of the holiday season have no part, or the senseless night-long parties that delight in wine-drinking. The wild celebration ends up as a drunken stupor, with everyone freely confiding the troubles of his love affairs. But love affairs and drunkenness are both contrary to reason, and therefore do not belong to our sort of celebrations. And as for all-night drinking parties, they go hand-in-hand with the holiday celebration and, in their wine-drinking, promote drunkenness and promiscuity. They are brazen celebrations that work deeds of shame. The exciting rhythm of flutes and harps, choruses and dances, Egyptian castanets and other entertainments get out of control and become indecent and burlesque, especially when they are re-enforced by cymbals and drums and accompanied by the noise of all these instruments of deception. It seems to me that a banquet easily turns into a mere exhibition of drunkenness. The Apostle warned: "Laying aside the works of darkness, put on the armor of light. Let us walk becomingly as in the day, not occupying ourselves in revelry and drunkenness, not in debauchery and wantonness."

Leave the pipe [*syrinx*] to the shepherd, the flute to the men who are in fear of gods and are intent on their idol-worshiping. Such musical instruments must be excluded from our wineless feasts, for they are more suited for beasts and for the class of men that is least capable of reason than for men. We are told that deer are called by horns and hunted by huntsmen to traps, there to be captured by the playing of some melody; that, when mares are being foaled, a tune is played on a flute as a sort of hymeneal which musicians call a *hippothorus*. In general, we must completely eliminate every such base sight or sound—in a word, everything immodest that strikes the senses (for this is an abuse of the senses)—if we would avoid pleasures that merely fascinate the eye or ear, and emasculate. Truly, the devious spells of syncopated tunes and of the plaintive rhythm of Carian music corrupt morals by their sensual and affected style, and insidiously inflame the passions.

The Spirit, to purify the divine liturgy from any such unrestrained revelry, chants: "Praise Him with sound of trumpet," for, in fact, at the sound of the trumpet the dead will rise again; "praise Him with harp," for the tongue is a harp of the Lord; "and with the lute [*cithara*], praise Him," understanding the mouth as a lute moved by the Spirit as the lute is by the plectrum; "praise Him with timbal and choir," that is, the Church awaiting the resurrection of the body in the flesh which is its echo; "praise Him with strings [*chordais*] and organ," calling our bodies an organ and its sinews strings, for from them the body derives its co-ordinated movement, and when touched by the Spirit, gives forth human sounds; "praise Him on high-sounding cymbals," which mean the tongue of the mouth, which, with the movement of the lips, produces words. Then, to all mankind He calls out: "Let every spirit praise the Lord," because He rules over every spirit He has made. In reality, man is an instrument made for peace, but these other things, if anyone concerns himself overmuch with them, become instruments of conflict, for they either enkindle desires or inflame the passions. The Etruscans, for example, use the trumpet for war; the Arcadians, the horn; the Sicels, the flute [*pectisin*]; the Cretans, the lyre; the Lacedemonians, the pipe [*aulos*]; the Thracians, the bugle; the Egyptians, the drum; and the Arabs, the cymbal. But as for us, we make use of one instrument alone: only the Word of peace, by whom we pay homage to God, no longer with ancient harp or trumpet or drum or flute which those trained for war employ. They give little thought to fear of God in their festive dances, but seek to arouse their failing courage by such rhythmic measures.

But make sure that the sociability arising from our drinking is twofold, in keeping with the direction of the Law. For, if "Thou shalt love the Lord thy God," and after that, "thy neighbor," then intimacy with

God must come first, and be expressed in thanksgiving and chanting of psalms. Only then are we free to show sociability toward our neighbor in a respectful comradeship. "Let the word of the Lord dwell in you abundantly," the Apostle says. But this Word adapts Himself and adjusts Himself to the occasion, person, and place; in our present discussion, He is the congenial companion of our drinking. The Apostle adds further: "In all wisdom teach and admonish one another by psalms, hymns and spiritual songs, singing in your hearts to God by His grace. Whatever you do in word or in work, do all in the name of the Lord Jesus, giving thanks to God His Father." This Eucharistic feast of ours is completely innocent, even if we desire to sing at it, or to chant psalms to the lyre [*cithara*] or lute [*lyra*]. Imitate the holy Hebrew king in his thanksgiving to God: "Rejoice in the Lord, O ye just; praise becometh the upright," as the inspired psalm says: "Give praise to the Lord on the harp [*cithara*], sing to Him with the lyre [*psalterion*]"—an instrument with ten strings—"Sing to Him a new canticle." There can be little doubt that the lyre [*psalterion*] with its ten strings is a figure of Jesus the Word, for that is the significance of the number ten.

It is fitting to bless the Maker of all things before we partake of food; so, too, at a feast, when we enjoy His created gifts, it is only right that we sing psalms to Him. In fact, a psalm sung in unison is a blessing, and it is an act of self-restraint. The Apostle calls the psalm "a spiritual song." Again, it is a holy duty to give thanks to God for the favors and the love we have received from Him, before we fall asleep. "Give praise to Him with canticles of your lips," Scripture says, "because at His command, every favor is shown, and there is no diminishing of His salvation." Even among the ancient Greeks, there was a song called the skolion which they used to sing after the manner of the Hebrew psalm at drinking parties and over their after-dinner cups. All sang together with one voice, and sometimes they passed these toasts of song along in turn; those more musical than the rest sang to the accompaniment of the lyre. Yet, let no passionate love songs be permitted there; let our songs be hymns to God. "Let them praise His name in choir," we read, "let them sing to Him with the drum and the harp." And the Holy Spirit explains what this choir is which sings: "Let His praise be in the church of the saints: let them be joyful to their king." And He adds: "For the Lord is well-pleased with His people." We may indeed retain chaste harmonies, but not so those tearful songs which are too florid in the overdelicate modulation of the voice they require. These last must be proscribed and repudiated by those who would retain virility of mind, for their sentimentality and ribaldry degenerate the soul. There is nothing in common between restrained, chaste tunes and the licentiousness of intemperance. Therefore, over-colorful melodies are to be left to shameless carousals, and to the honeyed and garish music of the courtesan.

Arnobius of Sicca

Arnobius of Sicca (d. ca. 330) taught rhetoric in the North African town of Sicca during the reign of the Roman emperor Diocletian (284-305). The date of his conversion to Christianity is not known, but his apologetical work, *Disputationum adversus gentes* (The Argument against the Pagans), was probably written during the first decade of the fourth century. Arranged in seven books, this work attempts to use the tools of pagan philosophy and rhetoric to prove the superiority of Christianity to pagan religions. In the extract from the seventh book given below, Arnobius pokes fun at the pagans for their employment of musical instruments to soothe or arouse their gods. Such use of instruments in pagan rites was reason enough for early Christians to banish them from their own worship.

From Arnobius of Sicca, *Disputationum adversus gentes*, VII, 32. *PL*, V, 1262. The English names of the instruments correspond to some form of the following Latin words: ringing of bronze = *aeris tinnitibus*; cymbals = *cymbalorum*; drum = *tympanum*; concord of sounds = *symphoniis*; castanets = *scabillorum*; pipe = *tibia*.

But it may appear to you that there is honor in wine and incense, and that the anger and displeasure of the gods are appeased by sacrifice and the slaying of victims. Are they also influenced by wreaths, garlands, and flowers? or the ringing of bronze and shaking of cymbals? or drums or concord of sounds? To what purpose is the rattling of castanets: that the deities might hear them, have respect to the performance, and forget their burning anger? Or, in the same way that the foolish crying of infants will be stopped when they hear rattles, are the almighty deities soothed by the shrill sound of pipes, and do they relax at the rhythm of cymbals, their indignation mollified? What is the meaning of those morning songs in which you add the pipe to your voices? Do they fall asleep up there and need to return to their vigils? Can you induce them to have a good sleep through lullabies or give them a pleasant wake-up call? Can you relax your audience to slumber by the use of soothing incantations?

Pseudo-Basil

The following extract from a commentary on the book of Isaiah, once attributed to Basil the Great (ca. 329-379) but now generally considered to be anonymous, suggests a direct connection between the playing of musical instruments and prostitution. The playing of the *cithara* and *aulos* are listed among the "useless arts" because there is nothing to show for them once the sound dies away. Significantly, the author did not include singing in this category, even though the same principle would hold true.

From *Commentary on Isaiah*, V, 158. *PG* XXX, 376-380. Translated by McKinnon in *Music in Early Christian Literature*, 70-71. A parenthetical reference by McKinnon to the original Greek word for *dancing* in the last sentence has been omitted in the present book.

'Woe', it is written, 'unto them who drink wine to the accompaniment of cithara, aulos, tympanum and song' (Is 5.11-12). You place a lyre ornamented with gold and ivory upon a high pedestal as if it were a statue or devilish idol, and some miserable woman, rather than being taught to place her hands upon the spindle, is taught by you, bound as she is in servitude, to stretch them out upon the lyre. Perhaps you pay her wages or perhaps you turn her over to some female pimp, who after exhausting the licentious potential of her own body, presides over young women as the teacher of similar deeds. Because of her you will meet with a double punishment on the day of judgment, since you are yourself immoral, and since you have estranged this poor soul from God through evil teaching. So she stands at the lyre and lays her hands upon the strings, her arms bare and her expression impudent. The entire symposium is then transformed, as the eyes of all are focused upon her and the ears upon her strumming; the crowd noise dies down, as the laughter and the din of ribald talk are quieted. All in the house are silenced, charmed by the lascivious song. (While he who is silent here is not silent in the church of God, nor does he listen quietly to the words of the Gospel. Not surprisingly! For that enemy who enjoins quiet there, advocates a disturbance here.) What a sorry sight for sober eyes that a woman weaves not but rather plays the lyre . . . Now among the arts which are necessary to life, the goal of which is plain to see, there is carpentry and the chair, architecture and the house, ship building and the boat, weaving and the cloak, forging and the blade; among the useless arts are cithara playing, dancing, aulos playing and all others whose product disappears when the activity ceases.

Epiphanius of Salamis

Born in Palestine, Epiphanius of Salamis (ca. 315-403) studied in Egypt—perhaps at Alexandria—returning to his homeland at the age of twenty and founding a monastery. About 367 he was named bishop of Salamis (Constantia) in Cyprus. According to his own testimony, he was brought up in the strict faith of the Council of Nicaea, and much of his life work was devoted to exposing and rooting out heresy wherever he found it. This pursuit led him into frequent and bitter controversy, even with such a noted adherent of the orthodox position as John Chrysostom. Epiphanius's most comprehensive writing against heresy was his *Panarion* (Medicine Chest), in which he described and attempted to provide antidotes for the "poisons" of eighty sects of his own and earlier times. Section XXV of the *Panarion* refutes the Nicolaitans, whom Epiphanius identifies as followers of Nicolaus of Antioch, one of the seven deacons mentioned in Acts 6:5. According to the *Panarion*, Nicolaus could not control his sexual appetites and, instead of ceasing his licentiousness, began teaching that such behavior was necessary to salvation. In the course of this discussion, Epiphanius refers to the *aulos* in unflattering terms as being symbolic of the serpent whom Satan used to tempt Eve and suggests a dark purpose behind the physical gestures and charming melodies of the *aulos*-player.

From Epiphanius of Salamis, *Panarion*, XXV, 4. *PG* XLI, 325-326. Translated by Frank Williams in *The Panarion of Epiphanius of Salamis, Book I (Sects 1-46)* (Leiden, the Netherlands: E. J. Brill, 1987), 80.

For there is a spirit of imposture which moves every fool against the truth with various motions, like breath in a flute. Indeed, the flute itself is a copy of the serpent through which the evil one spoke and deceived Eve. For the flute was prepared for men's deception, on the serpent's model and in imitation of it. And see what the flute-player himself represents; he throws his head back as he plays and bends it forward, he leans right and left like the serpent. For the devil makes these gestures too, in blasphemy of the heavenly host and to destroy earth's creatures utterly while getting the world into his toils, by wreaking havoc right and left on those who trust the imposture, and are charmed by it as by the notes of an instrument.

Gaudentius of Brescia

Details of the life of Gaudentius of Brescia (d. after 405) are very sketchy. A friend of Ambrose, he was appointed bishop of Brescia in northern Italy about 397. In 403 John Chrysostom was exiled by the Empress Eudoxia, and in 404-405, Gaudentius traveled to Constantinople at the request of Pope Innocent I to ask for Chrysostom's release, a mission in which he was unsuccessful. In one of his sermons, Gaudentius associates instrumental music with the lewd dancing at orgies, pleading with his listeners to keep themselves pure by avoiding such activities.

From Gaudentius of Brescia, *Sermo VIII. PL* XX, 890-891.

Otherwise, guard only against forsaking the faith, flee from fornication, be complete in faithfulness. You can hold on to this if you avoid drunkenness and degrading feasts, where the writhings of obscene women lead to illicit longings; where the lyre and tibia sound; finally, where all sorts of musicians make noise among the dancers' cymbals. Those are unhappy homes that are no different from theaters. I beg you to sweep away all this from among you. Let the home of the Christian and baptized men be innocent of the chorus of devils, let it be distinctly human, let it be hospitable; persistent in holy prayer; frequent in psalms, hymns, spiritual songs: let there be talk of God, and proof of Christ in the heart, in prayer, in countenance, during meals, during drinking, during conversation, in rising up, in lying down, in coming in, in going out, in joy, in sorrow; follow the teaching of the blessed Paul, "whether in eating, or drinking, or whatever you do, do all in the name of the Lord Jesus Christ, who called you by his grace" (1 Cor. 10).

4
The Organ in the Medieval Western Church

THE vehement and unanimous objections of the Church Fathers to musical instruments apparently succeeded in suppressing their use in Christian worship for many centuries. Indeed, as some of the writings in this chapter suggest, at least one instrument, the Greek hydraulic organ, appears to have been largely forgotten in the West. Besides falling under the general condemnation of instruments, the organ was particularly suspect because of its association with the Roman Colosseum—where early Christians had often been martyred—and thus no possible church use could have been contemplated. The organ was also relatively complex and expensive to build and maintain; there would be little use for such an instrument in a private household. Thus, unlike some instruments that—though not welcomed in the church—could still find a place in secular life, the organ fit into neither the religious nor the worldly sphere.

The demise of the organ as a common instrument in the West was so complete that when one arrived as a gift at the court of the Franks in 757 it was regarded as a great novelty. Although this particular organ had no association with the church, it was, relatively speaking, not long before monastic houses and churches began to see the usefulness of such fixtures. Organs began appearing in religious settings no later than the tenth century, by which time Christianity had been the dominant cultural force in Europe for over six hundred years; the earlier pagan associations of the instrument had long been forgotten.

Great care must be used when dealing with documents related to the presence and use of the organ in the medieval Western church. The most significant problem is the Latin word *organum* itself, which, as noted in the introduction to this book, can have a variety of musical and non-musical meanings. Furthermore, several writings that seemingly refer to organs in medieval church settings appear to be based on allegorical formulas used by the Church Fathers and other early Christian writers, suggesting that they are not to be taken literally. Finally, there are sometimes questions relating to the character of the organ itself: Was it mainly a musical instrument as is the case today? Or was it more like a siren—something that was merely intended to make a loud noise?

The last two problems cannot be dealt with directly here, though they should be borne in mind as the following passages are read. With regard to the first, a few documents will be found below that perhaps use the term *organ* in a generic sense, but most of the writings contain language that links the word directly with the modern understanding of an instrument with keyboards and bellows.

Einhard of Seligenstadt

Einhard (or Eginhard) of Seligenstadt (ca. 770-840) was of East Frankish origin and spent twelve years as a student at the monastery in Fulda, though he never became a priest or monk. About 793 he was sent by the abbot of Fulda to Aachen to study at the royal school of Charlemagne. His abilities in a number of fields quickly caught the eye of the emperor, who appointed him director of Royal Works for the court. Einhard's most famous writing was a biography of Charlemagne, written probably after 833. He also wrote a chronicle of major events in the kingdom of the Franks from 741 to 829. Among these events was the arrival of an organ in 757, a gift from the Byzantine emperor Constantine V to King Pepin of the Franks. The arrival of this instrument created a considerable stir. The organ sent by Constantine does not seem to have had any direct association with the church, but the appearance of this instrument at the court of King Pepin may be seen as an important step in the adoption of the organ by the Western church.

Einhard, *Annales* (757). *PL* 104, 377.

757

The Emperor Constantine sent many presents to King Pepin, including an organ; this reached him at the country seat in Compiègne, when he was holding a general assembly of the people. Tassilo, the leader of the Baioarians, also came there with the chief men of his nation, and after the manner of the Franks—their hands in the hand of the king in vassalage—commended himself, and promised fidelity to King Pepin and his sons Charles and Carloman, swearing upon the body of Saint Dionysius; not only that, but he also promised in a similar oath upon the body of Saint Martin and of Saint German the faithful service of the lords under his command during his lifetime. In the same manner also all the chiefs and elders of the Baioarian nation who had come with him into the presence of the king swore their faithful service to the king and his sons in the aforesaid venerable places.

In a later section of the *Annales*, Einhard notes the arrival at Aachen in 826 of a Venetian priest named George, who built an organ for the palace there. The organ that George built was a hydraulic instrument—probably modeled after the one that had been sent from Constantine to Pepin—and may have been the first organ constructed in the West during the Middle Ages. While again this was not a church organ, the presence of an organ builder at this time and place was an important step in the eventual introduction of the instrument into Christian churches.

From Einhard, *Annales* (826). *PL* 104, 502.

A certain Venetian priest named George, who claimed to be able to build an organ, came with Baldric; the emperor sent him to Aachen with Thancolf, the chaplain, ordering that they might be supplied with everything that was necessary for completing the instrument. And arranging for and proclaiming a general assembly for the middle of October, complete as usual in every custom, he departed across the Rhine with his retinue to the villa he called Saltz.

Einhard mentions George's instrument again in a book describing how he translated the relics of Saints Marcellinus and Peter from Rome to Seligenstadt in 827-828.

Einhard, *Historia Translationis BB. Christi Martyrum Marcellini et Petri*, VII, 75. *PL* 104, 583.

75. The seventh day before the kalends of August, a certain girl who was being vexed by an unclean spirit was brought into the church while the office of the holy oblation was being celebrated. Through the virtue of Christ and the merits of the blessed martyrs, the devil was put to flight and she recovered sanity of mind and wholeness of body. These are the miracles and virtues which our Lord Jesus Christ thought worthy to work through the merits of the holy martyrs Marcellinus and Peter in the town of Valenciennes, for the salvation of the human race: which the aforesaid priest George collected in a little book and took pains to send to us, and we thought to insert in this work of ours. This George is the Venetian who came from his country to the Emperor and with wonderful skill built an organ—which in Greek is called "hydraulic"—in the palace at Aachen.

William of Malmesbury

William of Malmesbury (ca. 1090-1143) was an English Benedictine monk and an author of historical and devotional works. Among his most important writings were the *Gesta regum Anglorum* (begun in 1118), a history of England from Anglo-Saxon times, and the *Gesta pontificum Anglorum* (completed 1126), a description of English church life during the same period. One portion of the latter work describes how Dunstan (ca. 924-988), the archbishop of Canterbury during the last fifteen years of the reign of King Edgar (ruled 959-975), built an organ for the use of the monastery at Malmesbury. Dunstan was largely responsible for reforming the monasteries at Malmesbury, Bath, and Westminster along strict Benedictine principles; he was well known in his own day as a metalworker, musical instrument maker, and painter. The Aldhelm mentioned in the extract given below was abbot of Malmesbury. Here, as in many medieval sources, the multiple manuals of the instrument led the writer to refer to the organ in the plural (organs), though only a single instrument is meant.

From William of Malmesbury, *De gestis pontificum Anglorum*, V, 4. *PL* CLXXIX, 1660.

Then, in the time of King Edgar, the most holy archbishop Dunstan directed with exceptional care the restoration and beautification of our monastery, inviting in love the holy Aldhelm and the neighboring West Saxon brothers: for this is the way the administration had been from the beginning, that the saint of the region might rejoice in repeated and frequent wonders, particularly in his times of exalted reflection. With much generosity to this place, Dunstan frequently conferred gifts which were of great wonder in England at that time, showing his virtue and genius. Among which I speak of excellent paintings and a mill; and organs, in which a bellows spews out troubled air through bronze pipes previously conceived according to musical measurements. Then he impressed this couplet on bronze plates:

The organs of the protector Dunstan for Holy Aldhelm
May the one who tries to remove them from this place lose the kingdom of eternity.

Wulstan of Winchester

Wulstan (or Wulfstan) of Winchester (d. 990) was a monk at St. Swithun's monastery, Winchester, and became a priest and cantor there. He wrote hymns, sequences, and tropes, as well as a life of St. Swithun, to which he prefixed a letter in hexameter verse addressed to Elfege, then the bishop of Winchester. The letter admires the building projects

Elfege had undertaken at Winchester, one of which was the installation or enlargement of an organ that was evidently of considerable size. Wulstan's description undoubtedly includes some elements of poetic license and symbolic interpretation, but it is valuable in that it seems to be based on direct observation by one who was probably a practicing musician. There can be little doubt that this was an unusual instrument for its time. The mention of the two brothers controlling their own alphabets perhaps refers to their writing the names of the notes on or above the keys; thus, *alphabet* is probably to be understood as *manual* in this context.

From Wulstan of Winchester, Letter to Elfege. *PL* I, 110-111.

Here you have made organs such as are seen nowhere else,
Set firmly on a double base.
Twelve bellows are joined together in order,
And below them lie fourteen more.
Very great winds are created by alternate blowings,
Which are powerfully stirred up by seventy men.
Many arms turning, and dripping with sweat,
They eagerly admonish one another:
"Lift with strength, push the air up,
Let it fill the entire box with a roar":
Which alone sustains 400 tones in order,
That are governed by the ingenious hand of the organist.
This opens the enclosures, and shuts them again
Raising up a variety of sound as determined by the melody.
Two brothers whose minds are in accord are seated,
And each is controller of his own alphabet.
Forty tongues hide the holes,
Each [tongue] governing ten [holes].
Some move forward, and others move backward,
Each keeping its proper place in the melody.
Seven intervals of the voices strike joy,
Mixing together in lyric semitones of song:
In an unyielding voice of thunder it strikes the ears,
So that except for this alone no other sound can be heard.
The noise is so loud, reverberating everywhere,
That everyone stops his open ears with his hands,
Not being able to bear the powerful roaring
Made by the clashing of the various sounds:

The melody of the songs is heard everywhere in the city,
Causing its fame to spread through the whole country.
This ornament of the church demonstrates your affection for the Thunderer,
And has been erected in honor of the holy key-bearing Peter.

Baldric of Dol

Baldric of Dol (ca. 1071-1131) was a native of Orléans, and a monk and abbot at Burguliensis. In 1095 he undertook a pilgrimage to the Holy Land, later writing a four-volume account of Jerusalem through 1099, when the city fell to the Crusaders. In 1114 Baldric was consecrated archbishop of Dol in northern France.

Sometime after his elevation to the archbishopric, Baldric made a visitation to the abbey of Fécamp, which possessed an organ. In a subsequent letter to the people of the town, Baldric mentioned seeing and hearing the organ, noting that it was played on at "certain times" and that the presence of this instrument had resulted in some criticism. Following in the tradition of the Church Fathers, Baldric gave an allegorical explanation of the organ, but whereas the earlier writers had intended such interpretations to deny the validity of instruments for Christian worship, Baldric's approach is employed in support of them.

Baldric, *Itinerarium sive epistola ad Fiscannenses*, VII. *PL* CLXVI, 1177-1178.

In this church was one thing that I esteemed greatly, that for the purpose of praising and calling upon God David inserted in his songs: "Praise," he says, "the Lord with strings and organ" (Psal. 150), inasmuch as I saw in that place a musical instrument constructed of bronze pipes, from which sweet music was produced by the exciting of workmen's bellows, and by a continuous diapason and symphony of sound low, medium, and high voices were joined, which might be thought to be the singing of a choir of clerks, in which boys, men, youths joined and continued in jubilation: they called this the organs, and played it on certain occasions. However, I am aware that there are many who have nothing like this in their churches, who cast stones at those who have them, murmuring against them and disparaging them, and we are not slow to add: they expose their ignorance of what the organs mean to us. They have forgotten that the psalter was written in lyrical poetry. They perhaps have not read that the most holy David soothed Saul's madness by gently playing the strings (1 Sam. 16). They certainly have ignored what Elisha, whose harshness had exasperated the king of Israel, ordered for himself:

"Bring me a harpist: while the harpist played, the hand of the Lord"—obviously the Holy Spirit—"came upon him" (2 Kings 3); his prophecy could not commence with an angry mind and an ill-disposed spirit. For this reason he entered into a trance through the service of a harpist. Thus, we do not wander from the path of so many of the fathers, but imitate them insofar as we can: not because we think God is pleased with these things, but through them many are joined into the heart of the church, like gold or silver or silken ornaments to the praise of God and the stirring up of the weakness of the human body. While I am not particularly delighted by the playing of the organs, I have the following interpretation: as many different pipes of various weight and size sound together by the agitation of one wind, so should men be of one mind, through the inspiration of the Holy Spirit, having the same will. Furthermore, when chopping unhewn logs or gathering unrefined stones, the work is made agreeable if you insist on being led by men of understanding: being united and not separated in their chopping and gathering, they join together with the cementing of charity. The organs that are placed in the church teach me all this: Is it not we who are the organs of the Holy Spirit? Finally, let whoever removes these from the church remove from the same all vocal sound and let him pray with unmoved lips, like Moses; you continue until the Lord says, "Why do you call upon me?" (Exod. 14). But if we do not suppress joy or the harmonious sound of voices, others may speak enviously, critically, or of how they disagree with the way it has been directed. We say that organs are perfectly acceptable, if they are interpreted mystically and we crave spiritual harmony from them; for the controller of all things has inserted this harmony into us, with many elements that are dissonant by themselves joined together and combined into fit rhythm. This is why I think organs, drums, cymbals, or the psaltery, and joyful voices are excellent: to be specific, that we may clearly and syllable by syllable reveal the Scriptures. Therefore, if we have organs, we are assured by the custom of the church; but if on the other hand we choose to do without them, we have committed no sacrilege. As we listen to the organs we are being united in spiritual harmony and cemented together with a double portion of love.

Aelred of Rievaulx

Not every medieval churchman was enamored with the increasing use of organs. One who was not was Aelred of Rievaulx (ca. 1110-1167). Born at Hexham, Northumberland, England, Aelred entered the Cistercian

Abbey of Rievaulx in Yorkshire about 1134 and became abbot there in 1147. He carried on an extensive correspondence and authored both ascetical and historical writings. His first significant work, *Speculum Caritatis* (The Mirror of Charity), was written through the encouragement of Bernard of Clairvaux. In the extract from this work quoted below, Aelred rails against some of the musical "vanities" employed in churches of his time, including polyphony, hocket (breaking up the notes of a single melody between two or more voices), and the use of organs and bells. Aelred, like Wulstan, takes note of the tremendous power of the organ. However, for the Aelred this was not a positive feature.

Aelred of Rievaulx, *Speculum Caritatis*, Book 2, Chapter 23, "De vano aurium voluptate." *PL* CXCV, 571-572.

The vanity of pleasing the ears.

Since we intend to exclude clearly evil persons from these considerations, the discourse may now turn to those who hide the business of pleasure behind a form of religion, who usurp for their own enjoyment of vanity the profitable method employed by the ancient Fathers as types of the future. Why, I ask, now that the use of such types and figures is ceasing, are there so many organs [*organa*] and cymbals [*cymbala*] in the Church? To what purpose, I beg you, is that awful blowing of pipes, more imitative of a crash of thunder than the sweetness of the voice? To what purpose is that contraction and breaking up of the voice? This one sings below, that one sings above; another in the middle divides and attacks some notes. Now the voice is constricted, now broken, now forced, now poured out to sound loud. Sometimes, it is shameful to say, it sounds like the neighing of horses; sometimes manly vigor is absent, the voice being given an edge of effiminate thinness; sometimes it is twisted and turned back by a type of artificial trill. Sometimes you can see a man with his mouth open as if to exhale before taking a breath, but without singing, as if to threaten silence by a ridiculous interruption of the voice, now imitating the agonies of death or the passion of suffering. Meanwhile, the whole body is agitated by histrionic gestures, the lips are twisted, the eyes rolled, the shoulders heave, and each note corresponds to the bending of fingers. And they call this ridiculous dissolution religion, and often, when they are thus agitated, it is claimed that they are thereby honorably serving God. Meanwhile, the crowd stands amazed at the sound of the bellows, the rattle of the cymbals, trembling and thunderstruck at the harmony of the pipes. These lascivious gestures in singing, the prostituting of voices through alternations and interruptions are greeted with jeering and laughter, such as one would expect to meet with in a theatre rather than a house of prayer, for the purpose of spectating, not for praying. They neither fear the terrible majesty that is near at hand nor regard the mystical cradle before which they minister, where Christ is being mystically enshrouded in bread, where his most holy blood is being released into the chalice, where the heavens are being opened and angels stand nearby, where the earthly is joined to the heavenly, and where angels are united with men. Thus, what the holy Fathers instituted that they might be awakened from infirmity to a state of devotion is being used for an unlawful practice of pleasure. Sound should not be preferred to understanding, but understanding accompanied by sound should generally elevate one to a higher state. Therefore, the sound ought to be orderly and serious, not twisting the soul to its own enjoyment, but giving to understanding the greater portion. For as the most blessed Augustine says (*Confessions*, x, 33), "The hearing of divine song moves the soul to a state of piety, but if the desire to hear the sound is greater than the understanding, it should be rejected." And in another place: "When I am delighted more by the song than the words, I confess that I have sinned, and prefer not to hear the singer." When, therefore, someone may scorn that ridiculous and destructive vanity, and apply himself to the ancient moderation of the Fathers, its noble dignity may cause his itching ears great loathing because he recollects such theatrical trifles and he thus despises and condemns as rustic behavior all the Fathers' seriousness in their mode of singing—which was instituted by the holy Spirit through the holy Fathers as his instruments [*organa*], namely Augustine, Ambrose, and especially Gregory—and he will prefer so-called Iberian lullabies or no telling what other vain trifles of some scholastics. If he is thus tortured, afflicted, or gasps anxiously after those things he has cast out, what, I ask, is the origin of this trouble, the yoke of chastity or the onus of worldly covetousness?

Sicardus of Cremona

Sicardus of Cremona (ca. 1150-1215) taught canon law at Paris, became a prebend at Mainz, and in 1185 was appointed bishop of Cremona. His *Mitrale*, completed by 1200, was one of the most influential medieval writings on the liturgy and served as a basic source for later authors, including William Duranti the Elder (ca. 1230-1296). The following extract from the *Mitrale* implies that organs (*organis*) and other instruments (*musicis instrumentis*) may have been played during Mass in the Hosanna section of the Sanctus. However, practically the same language is found in writings on the Sanctus by other authors, suggesting that Sicardus might have been merely following a conventional formula; the allegorical suggestion in the last sentence perhaps also indicates that the author was not speaking literally about a contemporary practice. Nevertheless, Sicardus's attitude toward instruments seems to be positive, based largely on the examples of David and Solomon. The context makes it clear that Sicardus was referring to the *organum* in its modern meaning, not in the sense of musical instruments in general.

From Sicardus, *Mitrale seu de officiis ecclesiasticis summa*, III. *PL* CCXIII, 123-124.

This Hosanna—a hymn which Pope Sixtus commanded to be sung at Mass—is repeated so that we may be counted among the angels with body and soul. And behold that occurs in this harmony of angels and of men whenever we use organs and musical instruments; this practice was begun by David and Solomon, who instituted hymns in the sacrifice of God to resound with organs and other musical instruments, and praises to be cried out by the people. But as the heart is greater than the body, the Lord may be more devotedly confessed with the heart than the body; for our singers are trumpet and psaltery, cithara and tympanum, choir, strings, and organ; and finally, loud sounding cymbals, as is sufficiently set forth at the end of the psalter.

Part III
The Sixteenth and Seventeenth Centuries

5
The Reformation and Counter-Reformation

THE Protestant Reformation of the sixteenth century presents a study in contrasts insofar as the use of musical instruments in the church is concerned. Some prominent reformers, such as Martin Luther, welcomed instruments into the church, appealing to the Old Testament and long-standing custom in the churches; others (e.g., John Calvin) vigorously opposed instruments in worship, calling the writings of Paul and the Church Fathers as their witnesses. By this time, instruments—especially the organ—were quite common in Roman Catholic churches, and no serious effort was made to banish them from the sanctuary, though some concern was expressed over the type of music that was played and other features of the instruments' use.

Martin Luther

While there had been numerous calls for a reformation of the church in the one hundred years before the birth of Martin Luther (1483-1546), it was not until his nailing of the ninety-five theses to the door of the Schlosskirche in Wittenberg that serious change became possible. Luther's aim was to reform the church, not to found a new one; thus, it is not surprising that he attempted to retain as much of the old form and practice as he could, in good conscience, accept. Essentially, Luther's philosophy regarding liturgical matters was that if a practice is beneficial to the spiritual life of the people and is not specifically condemned in the New Testament, it is acceptable. Thus, in his lecture on Psalm XXXII (33), he follows in the tradition of the Church Fathers by interpreting the musical allusions allegorically, but also notes that "God is to be praised . . . by . . . musical instruments." In the preface to his *Deudsche Messe*, Luther insists that the sounds of instruments are appropriate if they will help teach spiritual truths, especially to young people.

From Martin Luther, Lecture on Psalm XXXII (33). *WA* 3, 181. The bracketed phrases in the following extract are found thus in *WA*.

Some exult in the Lord[1] who rejoice in good spiritual health, whom the apostle encourages by saying, "brothers, rejoice in the Lord, again I say rejoice."[2] But these also are sorrowful in the world, because they are blessed who mourn.[3] For in the world they have trial, but in the Lord Christ peace. Wherefore 2 Cor. 1 says: "Who comforts us in all our tribulation."[4] Some, however, rejoice in the world, in the flesh, in the devil, in worse things, and rejoice themselves with the evil they will do (that is, in the doing of evil): This should not be understood that they rejoice because of the evildoing, but that their rejoicing is not in good works, but in evil, who rejoice in carnality. But of these the Lord says: "Woe to you who shall laugh now. For it will be, I say, that you shall weep." And again, "Woe to you who have your comfort here, etc."[5]

"It is fitting for the upright, etc." For though the perverse and incredulous—such as the Jews—may praise God, yet their praise is improper and unbecoming praise: But our God should have delightful and beautiful praise. Consequently, they are righteous who will not be led astray from right faith, as are the Jews, heretics, and the arrogant and lukewarm among the faithful. For the word of the Lord is right, as follows.

The "cithara"[6] is a musical instrument differing from the "psaltery" as follows: Both are of nearly the same shape—that of a triangle in the manner of the letter delta—except that the cithara [is an upright delta and] evidently resounds from the lower curved part of the instrument in which the strings are attached; the psaltery, however, [is an inverted delta], resounding from the curved upper part and with a stronger and better sound than the cithara. However, while these can be taken literally—since God is to be praised and is being praised today by both and many other musical instruments—yet it is appropriate that they be understood mystically, so that only God may be praised in relation to them, and not man. However, both are infinite mysteries.

---

[1]V. 1.

[2]Phil. 4:4.

[3]Matt. 5:4.

[4]2 Cor. 1:4.

[5]Luke 6:25, 24.

[6]V. 2.

From Martin Luther, Preface to *Deudsche Messe und ordnung Gottis diensts* (1526). *WA* XIX, 73.

However, it is not my intention that those who have prepared good [service] orders or who through God's grace can make a better one should abandon theirs and give way to ours. For it is not my view that all German lands must embrace our Wittenberg order. For even in earlier times the foundations, monasteries, and parishes were not alike in all things. But let the service be the same throughout a single district, and let the towns and villages use the same observance as the principal town; if other districts also adopt it or make use of it, let them do so freely and unaffectedly. In sum, we do not supply such orders for the sake of those who are already Christians; they have no need of such a thing, nor does one exist for the sake of it, but it exists for the sake of those of us who are not yet Christians, that they may be made Christians by us; their service of God is through the spirit. However, one must have such orders for the sake of those who may yet become Christians or be strengthened in their Christianity. For a Christian has no need of baptism, words, and sacraments, since as a Christian he already has them all, but he needs them as a sinner. But such are needed for the sake of the simple and the young people, who should and must be trained and educated daily in the scripture and the word of God, that they may dwell and rest in the scripture, be enlightened and knowledgeable in it, answer for their faith, and at the proper time teach others and help increase the kingdom of Christ; for the sake of such, people must read, sing, preach, write, and compose, and if it is helpful and conducive to growth, for that reason I would make all the bells to ring and all the organs to pipe, and use every sound that can sound. This is why the popish services are so damnable, because they have made laws, work, and merit out of them and thus the faith has been misrepresented and the young and simple have not been taught to exercise themselves in the scripture and the word of God, but they have become engrossed in the services and hold them to be useful and necessary to bliss; that is of the devil. The ancients themselves did not order or put such a thing in place.

Heinrich Bullinger

Huldreich Zwingli (1484-1531), the leader of the Swiss Reformation, was himself an accomplished instrumentalist, but his interpretation of the New Testament did not allow for the use of any music—including even congregational singing—in church. Besides being songless, this approach led to the silencing and eventual destruction of church organs in places that followed the Zwinglian model of church life. Heinrich Bullinger (1504-1575) succeeded Zwingli as chief pastor of the Swiss Reformed church at Zurich after the latter's death. Bullinger's most important writing was the second Helvetic Confession (1566), which became the official confession of faith of Reformed churches in Switzerland, Hungary, Bohemia, and other countries. In 1572 Bullinger completed his *Reformationsgeschichte*, a history of the Swiss Reformed church between 1519 and 1532. This work documents some of the occurrences of organ destruction by followers of Zwingli.

From Heinrich Bullinger, *Historia oder Geschichten, so sich verlouffen in der Eydgnoschafft, insonders zü Zürych mit enderung der Religion, und anrichten Christenlicher Reformation, von dem Jar Christi 1519 bis in das Jar 1532*. Source: J. J. Hottinger and H. H. Voegeli, eds., *Heinrich Bullingers Reformationsgeschichte* (Frauenfeld: Ch. Beyel, 1838), vol. 1, 161-162, 418, 437.

98. The reliquary and other known superstitions and abuses are done away with. . . . At this time [June, 1524] the magistrates of Zürich also ordered that in the city and churches there should be no more playing of the organs, tolling of bells for the dead or the weather, no more blessing of palms, salt, water, or candles, no more delayed baptism or extreme unction, but that people should completely cease and abstain from all these sorts of superstitions, since they are all contrary to the clear word of God. . . .

222. When the organs in the Zürich cathedral were demolished. Organs in the church are not of particular antiquity, especially in these lands. Since they also are not in accord with the Apostle's teaching in 1 Corinthians 14, the organs in the great cathedral of Zürich were demolished on the 9th of December in this year of 1527. Then people no longer desired either songs or organs in the churches. . . .

228. How the Mass and images were taken away in the city of Berne. The 22nd of January [1528] was the day of St. Vincent—who the city of Berne had anciently raised up as its patron—which the canons in Berne had maintained as a special feast, singing quite solemnly the evening Vesper. And when the organist was supposed to strike up the Magnificat, he played the song "O poor Judas, what have you done, that you have thus betrayed our Lord?" and this was the last song that was played on the organs. Soon after, the organs were demolished.

John Calvin

John Calvin (1509-1564) received a classical humanist training and studied for the law. He experienced a religious conversion at about age twenty-three and shortly thereafter was drawn to Protestant views, after which all his energies were directed toward preaching, writing, and directing the Genevan branch of the Reformation. One of the reformer's most significant books was the *Institutes of the Christian Religion*, a systematic theology that went through numerous editions and rewritings between 1536 and 1559. Calvin is also important for his influence in the development and spread of metrical psalmody in sixteenth-century Europe and America.

Whereas Luther's philosophy of worship was essentially that whatever was not specifically forbidden in the New Testament was acceptable, Calvin's approach was just the opposite: if a thing is not specifically commanded in the New Testament it is forbidden. Thus, though Calvin did not object to the private use of musical instruments, his views of them as a part of public worship essentially followed a familiar argument of the early Church Fathers: instruments were characteristic of the "infant church" (i.e., the Old Testament Jews), but their use constituted a ceremony that was no longer necessary in the New Dispensation. Like the Fathers, Calvin interpreted the instruments mentioned in the psalms and other Old Testament books allegorically. He also suggested that instruments constituted an "unknown tongue" and were thus to be excluded from worship. These beliefs are evident in Calvin's monumental commentary on the psalms, extracts from which are given below. Calvin's enormous personal influence led to the exclusion of musical instruments in the churches that followed his model of church life, including Reformed congregations in Geneva and the Low Countries, English and American Puritans and Separatists, and Scottish Presbyterians.

John Calvin, Commentary on Psalm 33. Source: Guilielmus Baum, Eduardus Cunitz, and Eduardus Reuss, eds., *Ioannis Calvini opera quae supersunt omnia* (Brunswick, Germany: C. A. Schwetschke et Filium, 1887), XXXI, 324-325. Translated by James Anderson in John Calvin, *Commentary on the Book of Psalms* (Edinburgh: Calvin Translation Society, 1845-1849), I, 538-539. Except where otherwise noted, the English names for the instruments in the following passages correspond with some form of the following Greek, Hebrew, and Latin words: cymbals = *cymbala*; harp = *cithara*; psaltery = *nebel*; tabret = *tympanum*.

2. Praise Jehovah upon the harp. It is evident that the Psalmist here expresses the vehement and ardent affection which the faithful ought to have in praising God, when he enjoins musical instruments to be

employed for this purpose. He would have nothing omitted by believers which tends to animate the minds and feelings of men in singing God's praises. The name of God, no doubt, can, properly speaking, be celebrated only by the articulate voice; but it is not without reason that David adds to this those aids by which believers were wont to stimulate themselves the more to this exercise; especially considering that he was speaking to God's ancient people. There is a distinction, however, to be observed here, that we may not indiscriminately consider as applicable to ourselves, every thing which was formerly enjoined upon the Jews. I have no doubt that playing upon cymbals, touching the harp and the viol [*nablum*], and all that kind of music, which is so frequently mentioned in the Psalms, was a part of the education; that is to say, the puerile instruction of the law: I speak of the stated service of the temple. For even now, if believers choose to cheer themselves with musical instruments, they should, I think, make it their object not to dissever their cheerfulness from the praises of God. But when they frequent their sacred assemblies, musical instruments in celebrating the praises of God would be no more suitable than the burning of incense, the lighting up of lamps, and the restoration of the other shadows of the law. The Papists, therefore, have foolishly borrowed this, as well as many other things, from the Jews. Men who are fond of outward pomp may delight in that noise; but the simplicity which God recommends to us by the apostle is far more pleasing to him. Paul allows us to bless God in the public assembly of the saints only in a known tongue, (1 Cor. xiv. 16.) The voice of man, although not understood by the generality, assuredly excels all inanimate instruments of music; and yet we see what St Paul determines concerning speaking in an unknown tongue. What shall we then say of chanting, which fills the ears with nothing but an empty sound? Does any one object, that music is very useful for awakening the minds of men and moving their hearts? I own it; but we should always take care that no corruption creep in, which might both defile the pure worship of God and involve men in superstition. Moreover, since the Holy Spirit expressly warns us of this danger by the mouth of Paul, to proceed beyond what we are there warranted by him is not only, I must say, unadvised zeal, but wicked and perverse obstinacy.

Commentary on Psalm 71. Baum et al., XXXI, 662-663; Anderson, III, 98.

22. I will also, O my God! praise thee. He again breaks forth into thanksgiving; for he was aware that the design of God, in so liberally succouring his servants, is, that his goodness may be celebrated. In speaking of employing the psaltery and the harp in this exercise, he alludes to the generally prevailing custom of that time. To sing the praises of God upon the harp and psaltery unquestionably formed a part of the training of the law, and of the service of God under that dispensation of shadows and figures; but they are not now to be used in public thanksgiving. We are not, indeed, forbidden to use, in private, musical instruments, but they are banished out of the churches by the plain command of the Holy Spirit, when Paul, in 1 Cor. xiv. 13, lays it down as an invariable rule, that we must praise God, and pray to him only in a known tongue. By the word truth, the Psalmist means that the hope which he reposed in God was rewarded, when God preserved him in the midst of dangers. The promises of God, and his truth in performing them, are inseparably joined together. Unless we depend upon the word of God, all the benefits which he confers upon us will be unsavoury or tasteless to us; nor will we ever be stirred up either to prayer or thanksgiving, if we are not previously illuminated by the Divine word. So much the more revolting, then, is the folly of that diabolical man, Servetus, who teaches that the rule of praying is perverted, if faith is fixed upon the promises; as if we could have any access into the presence of God, until he first invited us by his own voice to come to him.

Commentary on Psalm 81. Baum et al., XXXI, 760; Anderson, III, 312.

[3.] . . . With respect to the tabret, harp, and psaltery, we have formerly observed, and will find it necessary afterwards to repeat the same remark, that the Levites, under the law, were justified in making use of instrumental music in the worship of God; it having been his will to train his people, while they were as yet tender and like children, by such rudiments, until the coming of Christ. But now when the clear light of the gospel has dissipated the shadows of the law, and taught us that God is to be served in a simpler form, it would be to act a foolish and mistaken part to imitate that which the prophet enjoined only upon those of his own time. From this, it is apparent that the Papists have shown themselves to be very apes in transferring this to themselves. Under the new moon, by the figure synecdoche, is comprehended all the other high feasts. Sacrifices were daily offered; but the days on which the faithful met together at the tabernacle, according to the express appointment of the law, are called, by way of eminence, the days of sacrifice.

Commentary on Psalm 92. Baum et al., XXXII, 10-11; Anderson, III, 494-495.

In the fourth verse, he more immediately addresses the Levites, who were appointed to the office of singers, and calls upon them to employ their instruments of music—not as if this were in itself necessary, only it was useful as an elementary aid to the people of God in these ancient times. We are not to conceive that God enjoined the harp as feeling a delight like ourselves in mere melody of sounds; but the Jews, who were yet under age, were astricted to the use of such childish elements. The intention of them was to stimulate the worshippers, and stir them up more actively to the celebration of the praise of God with the heart. We are to remember that the worship of God was never understood to consist in such outward services, which were only necessary to help forward a people, as yet weak and rude in knowledge, in the spiritual worship of God. A difference is to be observed in this respect between his people under the Old and under the New Testament; for now that Christ has appeared, and the Church has reached full age, it were only to bury the light of the Gospel, should we introduce the shadows of a departed dispensation. From this, it appears that the Papists, as I shall have occasion to show elsewhere, in employing instrumental music, cannot be said so much to imitate the practice of God's ancient people, as to ape it in a senseless and absurd manner, exhibiting a silly delight in that worship of the Old Testament which was figurative, and terminated with the Gospel.

Commentary on Psalm 150. Baum et al., XXXII, 442; Anderson, V, 320.

3. Praise him with sound of trumpet. I do not insist upon the words in the Hebrew signifying the musical instruments; only let the reader remember that sundry different kinds are here mentioned, which were in use under the legal economy, the more forcibly to teach the children of God that they cannot apply themselves too diligently to the praises of God—as if he would enjoin them strenuously to bring to this service all their powers, and devote themselves wholly to it. Nor was it without reason that God under the law enjoined this *multiplicity* of songs, that he might lead men away from those vain and corrupt pleasures to which they are excessively

addicted, to a holy and profitable joy. Our corrupt nature indulges in extraordinary liberties, many devising methods of gratification which are preposterous, while their highest satisfaction lies in suppressing all thoughts of God. This perverse disposition could only be corrected in the way of God's retaining a weak and ignorant people under many restraints, and constant exercises. The Psalmist, therefore, in exhorting believers to pour forth all their joy in the praises of God, enumerates, one upon another, all the musical instruments which were then in use, and reminds them that they ought all to be consecrated to the worship of God.

Robert Holgate

The early English reformers seem to have been ambivalent about the role of musical instruments in the cathedral churches. (Instruments were seldom used in parish churches until the late seventeenth century.) Some cathedrals continued to make regular use of the organ, whereas in others the local ecclesiastical authority ordered them silenced. The two documents that follow were written by English bishops who opposed the continued employment of organs in the cathedrals under their authority.

Robert Holgate (ca. 1481-1555) became bishop of Llandaff in 1537 and archbishop of York in 1545. In 1552 he issued a set of Injunctions regarding various features in the life of York Cathedral, two of which forbade the playing of organs in the church.

Robert Holgate, "Injunctions given by Robert Archbishop of York to the Dean, Chapter and other ministers of the said Church containing the Comperts of his Grace's visitation kept within the Chapter House of his Cathedral Church of York the XVth day of the month of August in the year of our Lord God, 1552," Injunctions 24 and 25. Walter Howard Frere and William McClure Kennedy, *Visitation Articles and Injunctions of the Period of the Reformation*, Vol. XV of Alcuin Club Collections (London: Longmans, Green, 1910), II, 320.

24. *Also*, We will and command that there be no more playings of the organs, either at the Morning Prayer, the Communion, or the Evening Prayer within this Church of York, but that the said playing do utterly cease and be left the time of Divine Service within the said Church.

25. *Also*, forsomuch as playing of the organs ought and must be ceased and no more used within the Church of York, we think it meet that the Master of the Choristers for the time being who ought to play the same organs in times past who can no more so do, that the said Master of the Choristers do his diligence to his power to serve God in such

vocation as he can conveniently and may. Therefore we will and command that the said Master of the Choristers for the time being help to sing Divine Service to the uttermost of his power within the quire of the Church of York, specially of the Sundays and other Holy-days.

Robert Horne

Robert Horne (1514-1579) was made bishop of Winchester in 1561. In 1571 he issued a set of Injunctions for Winchester College, including one that ordered the silencing of the organ.

Robert Horne, "Injunctions given by the Right Reverend Father in Christ, Robert, by God's permission bishop of Winchester, to the Dean and Chapter Petit Canons Ministers Almsmen and other officers of the cathedral church of Winton the 2nd day of October in the year of our Lord God 1571 and of his consecration the eleventh," Injunction 27. Walter Howard Frere, *Visitation Articles and Injunctions of the Period of the Reformation*, Vol. XVI of Alcuin Club Collections (London: Longmans, Green, 1910), III, 330-331.

27. *Item*, that the organs be no more used in service time, and the stipend for the organ player and that which was allowed to a chaplain to say mass in the chapel in the Cloister shall be hereafter by the Warden and Fellows with the consent of the Bishop of Winchester turned to some other godly and necessary purpose in the college.

John Marbeck

John Marbeck (or Merbecke, ca. 1510-ca. 1585) served as organist at St. George's Chapel, Windsor, from at least 1531 until his death. In 1544, he was imprisoned for holding Calvinist beliefs, and though he was pardoned by Henry VIII and reinstalled in his organist's post, he had little enthusiasm for the position, having accepted the Calvinist arguments against instrumental music. Marbeck's most famous musical publication was *The Boke of Common Praier Noted* (1550), a setting of the Prayer Book service that had been authorized by the Act of Uniformity in 1549. In his *Booke of Notes and Common Places*, issued near the end of his life, Marbeck repeats familiar arguments that musical instruments were to be used only in the "infancy" of the church and that their continued use would constitute an "unknown tongue" such as was condemned by the apostle Paul. Much of the following passage appears to have been drawn from Calvin's commentary on Psalm 33 (as given previously). The first name in the passage is incorrectly given by Marbeck as "Tubal"; it was actually Jubal who was credited in Genesis 4:22 with the "invention" of music.

From John Marbeck, *A Booke of Notes and Common Places, with Their Expositions, Collected and Gathered out of the Workes of Diuers Singular Writers, and Brought Alphabetically into Order* (London: Thomas East, 1581), 754-755.

MVSICKE.

The first inuenter of Musicke.

TVbal[1] the sonne of Lamech by his wife Ada, inuented the science of Musick, by the stroke and noise of hammers of his brother Tubalkain which was a Smith.[2]

How farre Musicke is sufferable in holy assemblies

Praise the Lord vpon the harpe, &c.[3] ¶There is no doubt but that in this verse he expresseth the vehemencie & earnestnesse of his affection in praising God, when he will yt Musicall instruments shuld be applied to that vse. For he wold haue nothing by the faithfull that may kindle their minds & senses to set out the praises of God. For although Gods glory be not properly sette foorth, but by plaine vtterance of speach: yet is it not for naught that he hath added these helpes wherewith the faithfull are woont to stirre vp themselues, specially seeing he spake to the people of olde time. For there is a difference to be helde, that we drawe not to our selues, (without respect) whatsoeuer was commaunded the Jewes in olde time. And I am out of doubt for my parte, that the plaieng of Cymballes, singing to the Harpe and Viall, and all the whole order of Musicke, whereof mention is made oftentimes in the Psalmes, was a part of the lawe of schooling: I meane of the solempne furniture of the Temple. For at this daye, if the faithfull cheere vp themselues with instruments of Musicke, I saye their purpose ought to be, not to seuer their mirth from the praises of God. But when they haunt their holy assemblies, I think that musicall instruments are no more meet for ye setting forth of Gods praises, then if a man shall call againe sensing and lampes, & such other shadowes of the lawe. Foolishly therfore haue ye Papists borowed this & many other things of the Jewes. Men yt are giuen to outward pomps, delight in such noise, but God lyketh better the simplicitie which he commendeth to vs by his Apostle For Paule. 1 Cor. 14 suffereth not men to praise God in the open congregation of the faithfull, but with a knowne tongue. Certes the voice of man (although it be not vnderstood of all in

[1]Gen. 4.22

[2]Lanquet.

[3]Psa. 150.3

generall) farre excell all dead instruments[.] What shall we then saye of chauntinge, which onelye feedeth the eares with a vaine sounde: if anye man obiect that musicke, availeth greatly to the stirring vp of mens mindes: truely I graunt it doth so, howbeit it is alwaies to be feared least some corruption should creepe in, which might both defile the pure seruice of God, and also binde men with superstition. Moreouer, seeing that the holy Ghost warneth vs expresly of yt daunger by the mouth of Saint Paule: to proceede further then we haue warrant there, I say it is not onely an vnaduised zeale, but also a wicked stubburnenesse.[4]

Why the Musicall Instruments in olde time were vsed.

Bring forth the Tabret, the merrie Harpe with the Viall.[5] ¶The Leuites not without cause, vsed instruments of Musicke vnder the olde lawe, because it was Gods will to traine his people (which as yet were tender and childish) with such introductions untill the comming of Christ. But now when the brightnesse of the Gospell (hauing chased away the shadow of the lawe) betaketh to vs the seruice of God in a plainer sorte, we shall do but foolishly and lewdly to counterfeit that thing which the Prophet appointed onely for his owne time, whereby it appeareth that the Papists were right Apes, in conueieng ouer this thing vnto themselues.[6]

The Council of Sens

The Protestant Reformation provoked two reactions in the Roman Catholic Church: one a hardening of certain doctrinal positions and church practices, the other an attempt to reform some of the abuses of which the Protestants had complained. For example, at the Council of Trent, the structure of the Mass became standardized into a form that was basically invariable for the next four hundred years. On the other hand, popular accretions to the liturgy—such as the tropes and most of the sequences—were proscribed. The presence of musical instruments, particularly the organ, was apparently never seriously questioned, but the various councils and leaders sought to ensure that the instruments played music that was appropriate for the occasion. The Council of Sens (1528) was a local, not an ecumenical council, and thus its decrees were not applicable to the church at large but only to the immediate district. Nevertheless, the opinion expressed by the council on the organ is of

[4]Caluine.

[5]Psa. 81.3.

[6]Caluine.

considerable interest, for it made the claim that the use of the instrument was derived from the "fathers," though obviously this could not refer to the ancient Church Fathers. Furthermore, the council forbade the playing of secular music ("shameless or lascivious melodies") on the organ, implying that this must have been a common problem at the time.

From Concilium Senonense (1528), "Decreta morum," XVII. Giovanni Domenico Mansi, *Sacrorum Conciliorum* (Florence, 1759), XXXII, 1190.

The church received the use of organs in worship and divine service from the fathers. Therefore, we are unwilling that organ instruments should play shameless or lascivious melodies in the church, but only sweet sound, presenting nothing except divine hymns and spiritual songs.

Navarrus

Martin Aspilcueta (1493-1586), also known as Navarrus, was a Spanish professor of canon law at Toulouse, Cahors, Salamanca, and Coimbra. Widely regarded as a scholar and churchman in his own time, Navarrus's most significant work was the *Manuale sive Enchiridion confessariorum et paenitentium* (1588). In another work on the canonical offices, Navarrus accused organists of the time of playing "profane, and even vain and sometimes evil songs," and pointed out that the Credo and Gloria were often performed as organ solos, leading to the silence of the people and the choir or—even worse—to misbehavior in the latter group. Furthermore, the organists often played so long that the service was stretched out to unreasonable lengths. The identity of the "baxas" and "Atlas" songs mentioned in the following is not clear. A *baxa* was a type of shoe worn on the comic stage in ancient times, and the term might have been applied also to songs used in this venue; Atlas was the classical demigod who was doomed to support the world on his shoulders.

From Navarrus, *De horis canonicis*. Quoted in Martin Gerbert, *De Cantu et Musica Sacra* (San Blasien, 1774), vol. 2, 194-195.

Many organists frequently play profane, and even vain and sometimes evil songs in the church on the organ; of this sort are the ones they call "baxas," and "Atlas," and other songs that the people know to be filthy, obscene, and wanton. This is clearly sin, especially when they do this during the divine offices, because of the occasion it may present for diverting the mind's attention from divine and spiritual things and bending it to the temporal, vain, and evil. For this reason, in many places the *Credo* and *Gloria* are neither sung nor heard by the people at festivals; these are ordered not to be sung so that the pipes and harmonies may be heard. Instead of this, we should confess the holy catholic faith through heart and prayer, directing thanks to the Lord for his advent. Moreover, many organists, who display their skill so that they may be heard more fully, beat the keys so long (though this beating is no more than what one has called empty sound) that the Mass is protracted an hour too long. Such hearing so tires the people that it often introduces a great disdain for the assembly, the contemplation of the Redeemer's passion, and the redemption of humankind which is presented in that most holy consecration; thus, they think more about getting out of church than about its mysteries. Moreover, while the organs play, occasion is given for those in the choir to converse, joke, laugh, and carry on business; whenever they may think a little more on what the organs are playing, they think rather of the pipes than of what they themselves are doing or saying.

The Council of Trent

The most significant church council of the sixteenth century, the Council of Trent, met periodically between 1545 and 1563. The official decrees of the council seldom mentioned music; the chief instruction on this subject was issued in 1562. Like the Council of Sens, the participants in the Council of Trent accepted the use of the organ, only specifying that organists should not play anything that was "lascivious or impure."

From Council of Trent, "Decree Concerning the Things to Be Observed, and to Be Avoided, in the Celebration of Mass" (September 17, 1562). Source: Translated by J. Waterworth in *The Canons and Decrees of the Sacred and Oecumenical Council of Trent* (Chicago: Christian Symbolic Publication Soc., [1848]), 160-161.

In the next place, that irreverence may be avoided, each, in his own diocese, shall forbid that any wandering or unknown priest be allowed to celebrate mass. Furthermore, they shall not allow any one who is publicly and notoriously stained with crime, either to minister at the holy altar, or to assist at the sacred services; nor shall they suffer the holy sacrifice to be celebrated, either by any Seculars or Regulars whatsoever, in private houses; or, at all, out of the church, and those oratories which are dedicated solely to divine worship, and which are to be designated and visited by the said Ordinaries; and not then, unless those who are present shall have first shown, by their decently composed outward appearance, that they are there not in body only, but also in mind and devout affection of heart. They shall also banish from churches all those kinds of music, in which, whether by the organ, or in the singing, there is mixed up any thing lascivious or impure; as also all secular actions; vain and therefore profane conversations, all walking about, noise, and clamour, that so the house of God may be seen to be, and may be called, truly *a house of prayer*.

6
The Role of Instruments in Roman Catholic Spain and Italy

AS noted in the previous chapter, by the sixteenth century, organs had become common in the Roman Catholic church and their presence was not seriously questioned by the Counter-Reformation, though certain guidelines for their use were laid down by various writers. However, organs were not the only instruments that were found in Roman Catholic churches of the time, for as the writings in this chapter demonstrate, the instrumental ensemble sometimes played a significant role in the service. Indeed, the "a cappella" ideal of unaccompanied choral singing appears to have been largely an invention of the nineteenth, not the sixteenth, century. In addition to using orchestral instruments to double or substitute for the voices in choral works, Roman Catholic composers such as Giovanni Gabrieli wrote Masses and motets with specified instrumental parts, as well as strictly instrumental pieces for performance during the liturgy.

Francisco Guerrero

Francisco Guerrero (1528-1599) was one of the three great Spanish composers of the Renaissance period, the others being Cristóbal de Morales and Tomás Luis de Victoria. Apart from a brief stint as chapelmaster at the cathedral in Jaén, Guerrero spent his career at Seville cathedral, first as a singer and ultimately as prebend and chapelmaster. In the following document, he gives directions to the instrumentalists on how they should accompany the choir, in the course of the discussion mentioning the use of ornamentation ("glosses"), the instruments to be used, and when they are to play.

Francisco Guerrero, "Order Which Must Be Observed by the Instrumentalists in Playing" (July 11, 1586). From *Actos capitulares*, Seville Cathedral, Spain. Translated by Robert Stevenson in *Spanish Cathedral Music in the Golden Age* (Berkeley and Los Angeles: University of California Press, 1961), 167.

First, Rojas and López shall always play the treble parts: ordinarily on shawms. They must carefully observe some order when they improvise glosses, both as to places and to times. When the one player adds glosses to his part, the other must yield to him and play simply the written notes; for when both together gloss at the same time, they produce absurdities that stop one's ears. Second, the same Rojas and López when they at appropriate moments play on cornetts must again each observe the same moderation in glossing: the one deferring to the other; because, as has been previously said, for both simultaneously to add improvised glosses creates insufferable dissonance. As for Juan de Medina, he shall ordinarily play the contralto part, not obscuring the trebles nor disturbing them by exceeding the glosses that belong to a contralto. When on the other hand his part becomes the top above the sackbuts, then he is left an open field in which to glory and is free to add all the glosses that he desires and knows so well how to execute on his instrument. As for Alvánchez, he shall play tenors and the bassoon. At greater feasts there shall always be a verse played on recorders. At Salves, one of the three verses that are played shall be on shawms, one on cornetts, and the other on recorders; because always hearing the same instrument annoys the listener.

Adriano Banchieri

Adriano Banchieri (1568-1634) was a Benedictine monk who served as an organist at a number of Italian monasteries and churches. His compositions included both sacred and secular music, and he was also important as a writer on both musical and nonmusical subjects. One of his writings, the *Conclusioni nel suono dell'organo* (Bologna, 1609), contained instructions to organists on how to accompany a service. The practice of alternatim playing, in which the organ alternates with the priest, choir, or in some cases the congregation, receives prominent mention in the following extract from the *Conclusioni*. This type of performance was already well established in Roman Catholic churches, having been used for at least two centuries before Banchieri put these words down on paper.

From Adriano Banchieri, *Conclusioni nel suono dell'organo* (1609). Translated by William Klenz in *Giovanni Maria Bononcini of Modena: A Chapter in Baroque Instrumental Music* (Durham, N.C.: Duke University Press, 1962), 126-127.

Ninth Conclusion Explained

Regarding the Mass sung in alternation with the organ on the *canto fermo*. . . . On all feasts and Sundays of the year the Organ is played in Church . . . and here we shall treat of that which the organist should play in the Mass on the prescribed *Canto fermo*.

On all Sundays of the year, after tierce an Antiphon is sung as an Introit which begins *Asperges me Domine*, and when it is finished and repeated, the Introit [itself] is sung, to which, when the versicle *Sicut erat* a *ripieno* is played which serves as a reiteration of the Introit alternating with the Choir five responses to the Kyrie and Christe briefly.

The Gloria is intoned by the Priest with which alternation is made.

When the Epistle has been sung a *ripieno* or a *fugha* is played at [one's] discretion.

When the Alleluia and its verse have been sung one responds with the second Alleluia.

Regarding the Credo we will speak later in another place.

When the priest has sung *Oremus*, one plays until the prayers are over.

For the Sanctus one plays twice briefly.

For the Elevation [of the Host] one plays gravely, to induce devotion.

After the Pax Domini one plays a moment of [for?] the Agnus Dei.

When the second Agnus Dei has been sung by the Choir one plays a [*canzona*] *francese* or *aria Musicale*.

Special Notice

On Holy Thursday when the *Gloria in excelsis* has been intoned, a *ripieno allegro* is played, together with the bells.

On Holy Saturday when the Gloria has been intoned one responds as above. One does not play after the Epistle nor is the Credo sung. For the offertory and Sanctus one plays as has already been described, and similarly for the Elevation (there is no Agnus Dei).

After the Pax Domini one plays until the priest has finished communion.

Afterward the response attached to the Mass is sung by the Choir and one plays after the psalm *Laudate Domini omnes Gentes*.

For the canticle, *Magnificat*, one plays responses in the eighth tone, and at the end a *francescina allegra* [small canzona] and *Ite Missa est*.

The Credo of the Mass should be sung by everyone together for the greater devotion of the faithful . . . however, it is sung alternately with the organ at such times as when the organ & Organist respond with voices or when the choir is small in number when, while the Organ is played a Clerk reads the versicle in an understandable voice, notice that at the *Et Incarnatus est* one plays for the choir to sing it, for the genuflection.

Thomas Coryat

Thomas Coryat (ca. 1577-1617) was an English traveler whose *Crudities* relates his journey throughout much of the European continent. In the course of the work, he describes the music he heard at festivals in several Venetian churches and confraternities. It is quite likely that the famous second organist and composer of St. Mark's Cathedral, Giovanni Gabrieli—who was also one of the first composers to specify the instruments to be used in his church music—was associated with one or more of these events. Some of Coryat's descriptions fit nicely with the specified instrumentations of Gabrieli's *In ecclesiis* and *Quem vidistis*, late works that must have been composed about this time; while it cannot be unequivocally maintained that any of these pieces were performed on the occasions mentioned below, they were surely designed for just such presentation.

From Thomas Coryat, *Coryats Crudities Hastily Gobled up in Five Moneths Travells* (London: W. S., 1611), 249-253.

I was at three very solemne feasts in Venice, I meane not commessations or banquets, but holy and religious solemnities, whereof the first was in the Church of certaine Nunnes in St. *Laurence* parish, which are dedicated to St. *Laurence*. This was celebrated the one and thirtieth of Iuly being Sunday, where I heard much singular musicke. The Second was on the day of our Ladies assumption, which was the fifth of August being Fryday, that day in the morning I saw the Duke in some of his richest ornaments, accompanyed with twenty sixe couples of Senators, in their damaske-long-sleeued gownes come to Saint *Marks*. Also there were Venetian Knights and Ambassadors, that gaue attendance vpon him, and the first that went before him on the right hand, carried a naked sword in his hand. He himselfe then wore two very rich robes or long garments, whereof the vppermost was white, of cloth of siluer, with great massy buttons of gold, the other cloth of siluer also, but adorned with many curious workes made in colours with needle worke. His traine was then holden vp by two Gentlemen. At that time I heard much good musicke in Saint *Markes* Church, but especially that of a treble violl which was so excellent, that I thinke no man could surpasse it. Also there were sagbuts and cornets as at St. *Laurence* feast which yeelded passing good musicke. The third feast was vpon Saint *Roches* day being Saturday and the sixth day of August, where I heard the best musicke that euer I did in all my life both in the morning and the afternoone, so good that I would willingly goe an hundred miles a foote at any time to heare the like. The place where it was, is neare to Saint *Roches* Church, a very sumptuous and magnificent building that belongeth to one of the sixe[1] Companies of the citie. For there are in Venice sixe Fraternities or Companies that haue their seuerall halles (as we call the them [sic] in London) belonging to them, and great maintenance for the performing of those shewes that each company doth make; as that Fraternitie to whom this most portly building neare Saint *Roches* Church belongeth (being farre the fairest of all the sixe) doth enioy the yearely reuenew of foureteene thousand Chiquinies, which do amount to sixe thousand ninety fiue pounds sixeteene shillings and eight pence. Euery Chiquinie containing eleuen Liuers, and twelue sols; the Liuer is nine pence, the sol an halfe penny. So that the Venetian Chiquinie counteruaileth eight shillings eight pence halfe penny of our money. This building hath a maruailous rich and stately frontispice, being built with passing faire white stone, and adorned with many goodly pillars of marble. There are three most beautifull roomes in this building; the first is the lowest, which hath two rowes of goodly pillars in it opposite to each other which vpon this day of Saint *Roch* were adorned with many faire pictures of great personages that hanged round about them, as of Emperours, Kings, Queenes, Dukes, Duchesses, Popes, &c. In this roome are two or three faire Altars: For this roome is not appointed for merriments and banquetings as the halles belonging to the Companies of London, but altogether for deuotion and religion, therein to laud and prayse God and his Saints with Psalmes, Hymnes, spirituall songs and melodious musicke vpon certaine daies dedicated vnto Saints. The second is very spacious and large, hauing two or three faire Altars more: the roofe of this roome which is of a stately heigth, is richly gilt and decked with many sumptu-

[1]These Companies are neither more nor lesse then sixe to the end to answere the sixe parts or tribes whereof the whole citie consisteth; One Company being appointed for euery particular tribe.

ous embossings of gold, and the walles are beautified with sundry delicate pictures, as also many parts of the roofe; vnto this roome you must ascend by two or three very goodly paire of staires. The third roome which is made at one corner of this spacious roome, is very beautifull, hauing both roofe and wals something correspondent to the other; but the floore much more exquisite and curious, being excellently distinguished with checker worke made of seuerall kinds of marble, which are put in by the rarest cunning that the wit of man can deuise. The second roome is the place where this festiuitie was solemnized to the honour of Saint *Roch*, at one end whereof was an Altar garnished with many singular ornaments, but especially with a great multitude of siluer Candlesticks, in number sixty, and Candles in them of Virgin waxe. This feast consisted principally of Musicke, which was both vocall and instrumentall, so good, so delectable, so rare, so admirable, so superexcellent, that it did euen rauish and stupifie all those strangers that neuer heard the like. But how others were affected with it I know not; for mine owne part I can say this, that I was for the time euen rapt vp with Saint *Paul* into the third heauen. Sometimes there sung sixteene or twenty men together, hauing their master or moderator to keepe them in order; and when they sung, the instrumentall musitians played also. Sometimes sixteene played together vpon their instruments, ten Sagbuts, foure Cornets, and two Violdegambaes of an extraordinary greatnesse; sometimes tenne, sixe Sagbuts and foure Cornets; sometimes two, a Cornet and a treble violl. Of those treble viols I heard three seuerall there, whereof each was so good, especially one that I obserued aboue the rest, that I neuer heard the like before. Those that played vpon the treble viols, sung and played together, and sometimes two singular fellowes played together vpon Theorboes, to which they sung also, who yeelded admirable sweet musicke, but so still that they could scarce be heard but by those that were very neare them. These two Theorbists concluded that nights musicke, which continued three whole howers at the least. For they beganne about fiue of the clocke, and ended not before eight. Also it continued as long in the morning: at euery time that euery seuerall musicke played, the Organs, whereof there are seuen faire paire in that roome, standing al in a rowe together, plaied with them. Of the singers there were three or foure so excellent that I thinke few or none in Christendome do excell them, especially one, who had such a peerelesse and (as I may in a maner say) such a supernaturall voice for sweetnesse, that I thinke there was neuer a better singer in all the world, insomuch that he did not onely giue the most pleasant contentment that could be imagined, to all the hearers, but also did as it were astonish and amaze them. I alwaies thought that he was an Eunuch, which if he had beene, it had taken away some part of my admiration, because they do most commonly sing passing wel; but he was not, therefore it was much the more admirable. Againe it was the more worthy of admiration, because he was a middle-aged man, as about forty yeares old. For nature doth more commonly bestowe such a singularitie of voice vpon boyes and striplings, then vpon men of such yeares. Besides it was farre the more excellent, because it was nothing forced, strained, or affected, but came from him with the greatest facilitie that euer I heard. Truely I thinke that had a Nightingale beene in the same roome, and contended with him for the superioritie, something perhaps he might excell him, because God hath granted that little birde such a priuiledge for the sweetnesse of his voice, as to none other: but I thinke he could not much. To conclude, I attribute so much to this rare fellow for his singing, that I thinke the country where he was borne, may be as proude for breeding so singular a person as *Smyrna* was of her *Homer*, *Verona* of her *Catullus*, or *Mantua* of *Virgil*: But exceeding happy may that Citie, or towne, or person bee that possesseth this miracle of nature. These musitians had bestowed vpon them by that company of Saint *Roche* an hundred duckats, which is twenty three pound sixe shillings eight pence starling. Thus much concerning the musicke of those famous feastes of S. *Laurence*, the Assumption of our Lady, and Saint *Roche*.

Michael Praetorius

Michael Praetorius (ca. 1571-1621) was born in Creuzburg, Germany. About 1587 he became organist of St. Marien Church, Frankfurt, holding this post for three years. Subsequently, he served as organist and chapel-master at the court of Duke Heinrich Julius of Brunswick-Wolfenbüttel. After the duke's death he spent much time in Dresden, though still nominally employed by Heinrich Julius's son.

Praetorius was a prolific composer, particularly of choral music based on Lutheran chorales. Of equal—if not greater—significance was his *Syntagma musicum* (1614-1620), a three-volume work that provides much information on the theory and practice of music in the late sixteenth and early seventeenth centuries. Three extracts from the third volume of *Syntagma musicum* (1619) are given here. The first discusses the meaning of the term "capella" as used in contemporary Italian practice, with special reference to the music of Giovanni Gabrieli. (The 1597 work by Gabrieli referred to in the following as *Cantiones sacrae* was actually titled *Symphonia sacrae.*) Though Praetorius was a German Protestant, and made frequent reference to his own compositions in this volume of *Syntagma musicum*, the practices he described were derived mainly from Italian music of the time. The word *concerto* as used below does not refer to a multimovement work for solo instrument(s) and orchestra, as in the eighteenth through twentieth centuries, but to a relatively short sacred work for choir, soloists, and instruments, or some combination of these.

From Michael Praetorius, *Syntagma musicum*, vol. 3 (Wolfenbüttel: Elias Holwein, 1619), 133-135.

Chapter 2.

Capella, Chorus pro Capella, Palchetto

The word capella can be found in three correct senses.

1. It is my opinion that the Italians originally understood this to refer solely to the practice of the Imperial, Austrian, and other large Catholic chapels and "musics" in which a single choir is drawn out of several distinct choirs containing all kinds of instruments and men's voices. Called a *chorus pro capella*, because it is performed by the whole vocal choir or *capella*, this choir is separated from the others and joins in with them in a manner similar to the full *Werk* on an organ. This gives an excellent embellishment, magnificence, and glow to such music, because this choir generally joins in when the other choirs all come together.

And the harmony and magnificence will be further filled up and expanded when one arranges for a large bass pommer, double bassoon, or large bass viol (in Italian, *Violone*), as well as other instruments where they are available, to be distributed among the middle and upper parts. One, two, or three different such *capellas* can be taken out of every concerto—each consisting of four or more persons, when one can have them—and placed in separate parts of the church. Furthermore, if things are such that not enough persons are available, the *capella* can be wholly and completely omitted, since the *capella*, almost like the *ripieno*, is extracted and drawn out from the other choirs solely for the filling up and reinforcement of the music, a derived choir; in these, unisons and octaves are composed without discrimination, the reasons and causes of which are set forth in the twelfth chapter of part two.

And I have seen many different such *capellas* in copies of some of Giovanni Gabrieli's concertos; however, they do not appear in those newly printed last year.

2. However, in Gabrieli's *Cantiones sacrae* first published in the year 1597, the word *capella* is found often and means the same thing as what I call *chorus vocalis* or *chorus vocum*; that is, the choir that must contain singers and men's voices. For example, a concerto may have one choir containing cornetts, another with violins, and a third with trombones, bassoons, flutes, and similar instruments, but each will include at least one man's voice. However, there is usually one choir in which all four parts are set for singers; G. Gabrieli calls this choir the *capella*. And such a choir or *capella* should never be omitted, because it belongs among the principal choirs. The *capella* can be recognized easily by the clefs, and can be accompanied with viola da gamba or viola da braccio. A detailed discussion of this will follow in chapter eight.

In my concertos—particularly the Latin ones but also some of those in German—in which I did not wish to use a *chorus pro capella*, I have usually marked the words *omnes*, *solus*, or *voce*, *instrumento*, *trombone*, etc., nearby, which is easy for anyone to understand and arrange for themselves. Furthermore, where *voce* and *trombone* or *voce* and *violino* appears, both a vocalist and a trombonist or violinist must be included. Where only *voce* is found, the vocalist sings by himself; where *trombone*, the trombonist goes alone; where *omnes*, both musicians perform together. The same approach is taken when other kinds of instruments are called for. And anyone can draw out at his pleasure one or two *capellas* of four voices not only from works that are divided in this manner, but also from all other concertos, if enough singers and instrumentalists are available, and where the words *omnes* or *chorus* are marked, or where all the choirs join together, or where it is otherwise appropriate, writing them out on a separate sheet (as is fully indicated in the twelfth chapter of part two). Following the word *solus*, *voce*, *instrumento*, etc., the proper number of rests must be placed. The *chorus pro capella* is arranged and placed in a separate place from the other musicians.

Some years ago I already began to use the words *omnes* and *solus* in my *Cantionibus*. Now, however, I find that in their concertos the Italians use the word *ripieno*.

3. Finally, however, some also call it a *capella* when one composes an instrumental choir and adds it to a vocal choir. This instrumental choir does not contain the principal parts and can be left out if instrumentalists are lacking; the piece can be performed by the vocal choir alone without instrumentalists—except for an organist with a positif or

regal—since it contains the principal parts. The instrumental choir should be separated from the vocal choir, perhaps opposite to it or on a higher or lower place. In Italy this is also called a *palchetto*, for they may use more than one choir *pro capella* and always place one over the other, just as in David's time the temple musicians were apparently divided and placed in different higher and lower choirs. Thus, some special psalms—such as the 120th through the 134th—are called songs for the higher choir, as can be seen at length in volume one, part one, section one, chapter two.

However, the meaning of the word *palchetto* can better be understood from the following brief description. In some churches and princely chapels, at ground level or at another convenient place where the musicians can remain unhindered by the listeners, a platform of beams and boards is constructed—such as is found in a theatre—or laid over some seats to which supports are added and dressed up with tapestries. If desired, one can also erect a special raised platform—like a small *Borkirche*—with different choirs placed separately from the others. Places that are convenient for this purpose are found in many old churches, and especially back in the choirs, and these can thus be called *palchetto*.

In the second extract, Praetorius gives instructions regarding the improvisation of an organ prelude before the performance of a concerto or motet (Praetorius, *Syntagma musicum*, 151-152). This passage suggests that the organ prelude was sometimes used as an opportunity for other instrumentalists to tune their instruments. The word *cornett* is used in the following as a translation of the German *Zink*. The translations of other instrument names follow standard modern terminology.

In conclusion, however, I must give here a friendly instruction to the organists when they perform a concerto with several choirs in the church or at the table. Like excellent orators, when they attempt important subjects and wish to expound upon them, organists should generally append an introduction to the piece, though it is not an integral part of the work. This will make the hearers give close attention, be ready to listen, and stay alert. These opening preludes will bring together the listeners and the whole consort of musicians, who will search out their parts and tune their instruments, and thus prepare for the beginning of a good and well-sounding music.

However, since lutanists and violists usually begin tuning their lutes and violins on G, it is necessary that they first touch the octaves on G with both hands, remaining on this note a little while, then dampening it. Afterwards, they should follow with D, then A, E, C, and F, playing each one with the left hand for two or three beats, then dampening it. If they like, they may play elegant running passages and other diminutions with the right hand, as is customary in toccatas. They continue until the others have taken out and tuned their lutes, violas, and violins, etc., and then they are able to begin a little fugue, a lovely fantasia, or a toccata. After a short while, they break off on the final of the key in which the concerto begins so that they can establish it with a good grace, and then the full number of the entire consort can in God's name begin a good concerto, motet, madrigal, or pavane.

However, it causes a very great inconvenience and noise if the instrumentalists tune their bassoons, trombones, and cornetts in the middle of the organist's prelude, making many pipings and fussings, so that one's ears hurt and the listeners get the shivers. This sounds so bad and makes such a racket that a person might think he has been stung or cut. Therefore, let the cornett and trombone players tune their instruments and warm up their mouthpieces in private before they are called upon to appear in the church or somewhere else. Thus, such dissonances and awful sounds will not offend the ears and spirits of the hearers, but will rather bring them delight.

The final extract from Praetorius's *Syntagma musicum* describes the method for determining the instrumentation to be used in an ostensibly "a cappella" piece (152-154).

Chapter VII.

A method by which each concerto and motet can be arranged for all sorts of instruments and men's voices quickly and without great difficulty, whether it has few or many choirs.

Though I could perhaps have already given a somewhat more detailed description of the method by which one can arrange every vocal concerto for various instruments, I have left consideration of it to the present time. For music has made such great progress here that more excellent musicians are now found in our country of Germany, as is shown not only by the magnificent and lovely German and Latin concertos that have appeared in public print, but also by the fact that these musicians know better how to arrange and direct these choral concertos than I can describe in my present little writings.

But to speak briefly, I have adopted the following method, which no one else has used, of writing down one after another the clefs of each part in an author's concerto, as I have done in the basso continuo of my *Polyhymnia*, in which I noted down in an orderly succession in the back the clefs of all the parts for each song. This reflects the character of the whole concerto like a mirror, in which it will be observed how high and low each part ascends or descends according to the tone or mode in which the song is composed, and thus what wind or string instruments are fit for each part, and which choir should be designated *capella* and include singers. As an example, I will set before you some motets by Orlando di Lasso that are known everywhere.

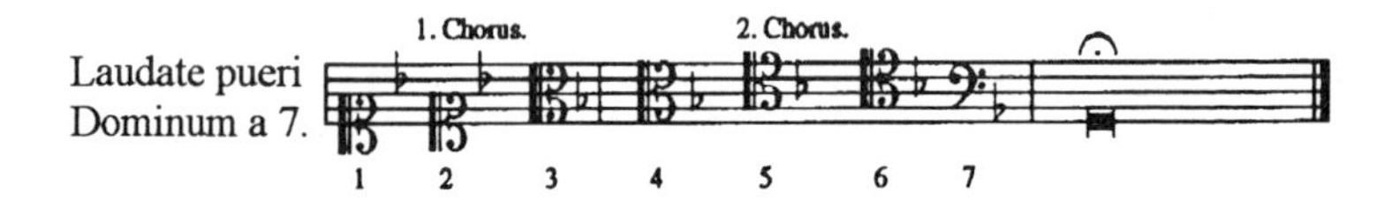

From this it can be seen immediately that—when instrumentalists are available—the two discant parts should be played on two transverse flutes, two treble violins, or two cornetts, but the alto (which serves as the bassett of this choir) should be performed by the human voice. In the other choir, the alto (which serves as the cantus of this second choir) should also be performed by the human voice; however, the two tenor parts and the bass must be arranged for and played upon three trombones.

In the first choir one can quite fittingly arrange and place three transverse flutes, three muted cornetts, or three violins, or the parts can be distributed in successive order to a mixed ensemble of one violin, one cornett, and one transverse flute or recorder. However, the bassett must be sung by a tenor, which, if one wishes, can be doubled by a trombone; the part will also sound well if played on a trombone or bassoon without the human voice, in which case one of the discant parts should be sung by a boy so that the words can be heard. In the other choir, one may use only voices, or violin da gamba, violin da braccio, or recorders, besides a bassoon or bass trombone. However, either the discant or tenor parts—or both—must be sung by the human voice, whether or not they are doubled by the instruments.

Amante Franzoni

Little is known about the life of Amante Franzoni (d. ca. 1630), except that he was born in Mantua, where he seems to have lived and worked most of his life, apart from a brief stint in Forli. The table of contents of his *Apparato Musicale* (1613) is significant because it mentions the roles of independent instrumental works as substitutes or introductions for vocal performance of certain portions of the Mass.

From Amante Franzoni, *Apparato Musicale di Messa, Sinfonie, Canzoni, Motetti, & Letanie della Beata Vergine* (Venice: Ricciardo Amadino, 1613), Table of Contents. Claudio Sartori, *Bibliografia della Musica Strumentale Italiana stampata in Italia fino al 1700* (Florence, Italy: Leo S. Olschki, 1952), 188.

TAVOLA DI QUANTO SI CONTIENE NELLA presente Opera.

Carlo Milanuzzi

Carlo Milanuzzi (d. ca. 1647) was an Augustinian monk who served as organist or *maestro di cappella* at Italian churches in Venice, Perugia, Verona, Modena, and Camerino. Like the work by Franzoni noted above, the table of contents of Milanuzzi's *Armonia Sacra* (1622) lists the liturgical function of the instrumental pieces in the collection.

Carlo Milanuzzi, *Armonia Sacra di Concerti, Messa, & Canzoni à cinque voci con il suo Basso Continuo per l'Organo* (Venice: Alessandro Vincenti, 1622), Table of Contents. Sartori, *Bibliografia della Musica Strumentale*, 282.

TAVOLA DELL'ARMONIA SACRA.DI CARLO MILANUZII.

Concerto A 5.	Per l'Introito.	1
Messa Liquide perle Amor A 5.		2
Canzon A 5. detta la Zorzi.	Per l'Epistola.	5
Concerto A 5.	Per l'Offertorio	10
Concerto à due Canti, ò Tenori.	Per l'Eleuatione.	12
Canzon A 5. detta la Riatelli.	Per il Post Comunio.	14
Canzon A 2. all Bastarda	Per il Trôbone, e Violino. Per il Deo Gratias.	16

7
The English Church in the Seventeenth Century

ORGANS did not generally find their way into English parish churches until after the middle of the seventeenth century, perhaps due in part to the objections of reformers such as Holgate, Horne, and Marbeck. In addition, organs and organists were expensive to secure and maintain. However, once the Anglican church was firmly established during the reign of Elizabeth I (queen 1558-1603), most English cathedrals continued or returned to the use of organs. In 1640 King Charles I called the Long Parliament to secure finances for his attempt to suppress rebellion in Scotland. However, Parliament was dominated by Puritans, and civil war soon broke out between Royalists and Parliamentarians. The forces of Charles I were defeated and in 1649 he was beheaded, ushering in the Puritan Commonwealth under Lord Protector Oliver Cromwell (1599-1658). The Puritans adhered to the Calvinist belief that musical instruments and other "popish" ornaments had no place in Christian worship, and during the war many cathedrals were defaced and their organs destroyed, though much of this damage probably resulted from unruly soldiers rather than an organized campaign of destruction. The restoration of the English monarchy under Charles II in 1660 reversed the trend of the Commonwealth years, and the use of organs began to spread in cathedral and parish churches alike.

Bruno Ryves

One of the chief sources of information about the destruction of organs by Puritan (Roundhead) troops is a book by Bruno Ryves (1596-1677), *Mercurius Rusticus*. Ryves's account should be handled with some caution; the author was a confirmed Royalist, and his book was not published until over forty years after the events that it purportedly describes.

From [Bruno Ryves], *Mercurius Rusticus: or, the Countries Complaint of the Sacrileges, Prophanations, and Plunderings, Committed by the Schismatiques, on the Cathedral Churches of This Kingdom* (London, 1685), 119-120 (extract from a letter dated August 30, 1642, from Thomas Paske, subdean of Canterbury Cathedral, to the Earl of Holland regarding the behavior of Roundhead troops in Canterbury Cathedral).

Colonel Sandys *arriving here with his Troops, on Friday night, presently caused a strict watch and Sentinels to be set both upon the Church, and upon our several houses, to the great affright of all the Inhabitants: this done, Sergeant Major* Cockaine *came to me, and in the name of the Parliament, demanded to see the Arms of the Church, and the Store-powder of the County, which I presently shewed him; when he possessed himself of the Keys, and keep them in his own custody: the next morning we were excluded the Church, and might not be permitted to enter, for the preformance of our divine Exercises, but about eight of the Clock, Sir* Michael Livesey *attended with many Soldiers, came unto our Officers, and commaded them, to deliver up the keys of the Church, to one of their Company, which thoy did, and thereupon he departed, when the Soldiers entering the Church, and Quire, Giant-like, began a fight with God himself, overthrew the Communion-Table, tore the Velvet cloth from before it, defaced the goodly Screen, or Tabernacle-work, violated the Monuments of the Dead, spoyled the Organs, brake down the ancient Rails, and Seats, with the brazen Eagle which did support the Bible, forced open the Cupboords of the Singing-men, rent some of their Surplices, Gowns and Bibles, and carryed away others, mangled all our Service-books, and Books of Common-Prayer; bestrwing the whole Pavement with the leaves thereof: a miserable spectacle to all good eyes: but as if all this had been too little, to satisfied the fury of some indiscreet zealots among them (for many did abhor what was done already) they further exercised their malice upon the Arras hanging in the Quire, representing the whole story of our Saviour, wherein observing divers figures of Christ, (I tremble to express their blasphemies) one said that here is Christ, and swore that hee would stab him: another said here is Christ, and swore that he would rip up his Bowels: which they did accordingly, so far as the figures were capable thereof, besides many other Villanies: and not content therewith, finding another statue of Christ in the Frontispiece of the South-gate, they discharged against it forty shot at the least, triumphing much, when they did hit it in the head, or face, as if they were resolved to crucifie him again in his figure, whom they could not hurt in truth: nor had their fury been thus stopped, threatning the ruine of the whole Fabrick, had not the Colonel, with some others, come to the relief and rescue: the Tumults appeased, they presently departed for* Dover, *from whence we expect them this day; and are much afraid, that as they have already vilified our Persons, and offered extream indignity to one of our Brethren, so they will Plunder our Houses at their Return, unless the care of the Major, the Colonel, and some Members of the House of Commons (Sir* Edward Masters, *and Captain* Nut, *now with us, who have promised to present their knowledg to that honourable House) do prevent the same.*

The destruction of the organ at Chichester Cathedral (ibid., 139).

To this purpose, the Rebels under the Conduct of Sir *William Waller*, entering the City of *Chichester* on *Innocents* day, 1642. the next day, their first business was to Plunder the Cathedral Church; the Marshal therefore and some other Officers having entred the Church went unto the Vestery, where they seize upon the Vestments and ornaments of the Church, together with the Consecrated Plate, serving for the Altar, and administration of the Lords Supper: they left not so much as a Cushion for the Pulpit, nor a Chalice for the Blessed Sacrament: the Commanders having in person executed the *covetous part* of Sacrilege, they leave the *destructive* and *spoyling part* to be finished by the Common Soldiers: brake down the Organs, and dashing the Pipes with their Pole-axes, scoffingly said, *hark how the Organs go.*

The destruction of the organ at Westminster Abbey (ibid., 153-154).

This Church, under the eye, and immediate protection of the pretended Houses of Parliament, had its share in spoil, and prophanation, as much as those Cathedrals, which were more remote from them: for in *July* last, 1643. some Soldiers of *Weshborne*, and *Cacwoods* Companies (perhaps because there were no Houses in *Westminster*) were quartered in the *Abby Church*, where (as the rest of our Modern Reformers) they brake down the Rail abut the Altar, and burnt it in the place where it stood: they brake down the Organ, and pawned the Pipes at several Ale-houses for Pots of Ale: They put on some of the singing mens Surplesses, and in contempt of the Canonical Habit, ran up and down the Church, he that wore the Surpless, was the Hare, the rest were the Hounds.

The Long Parliament

The destruction of English church organs was given official sanction by the Long Parliament in a 1644 ordinance, the text of which is given below.

"An Ordinance for the further demolishing of Monuments of Idolatry, and Superstition" (May 9, 1644). Source: *Two Ordinances of the Lords and Commons Assembled in Parliament, for the Speedy Demolishing of All Organs, Images, and All Manner of Superstitious Monuments in All Cathedrall Parish Churches and Chappels, throughout the Kingdom of England and Dominion of Wales* (London: John Wright, 1644), 3-4.

The Lords and Commons assembled in Parliament, the better to accomplish the blessed Reformation so happily begun, and to remove all offences and things illegall in the worship of God, do Ordaine, That all representations of any of the persons of the Trinity, or of any Angell, or Saint, in or about any Cathedrall, Collegiate, or Parish Church, or Chappell, or in any open place within this Kingdome, shall be taken away, defaced, and utterly demolished; And that no such shall hereafter be set up, And that the chancell-ground of every such church or chappel raised for any Altar, or communion-table to stand upon, shall be layd down and levelled; And that no Copes, Surplisses, superstitious Vestments, Hoods, or Roodlofts, or holy-Water Fonts, shall be, or be anymore used in any Church or Chappel within this Realme; And that no crosse, crucifix, picture, or Representation of any of the persons of the Trinity, or of any Angel or Saint shall be or continue upon any plate or other thing used, or to be used in or about the worship of God; And that all Organs, and the frames or cases wherin they stand in all Churches and Chappels afresaid shall be taken away, and utterly defaced, and none other hereafter set up in their places; And that all Copes, Surplisses, superstitious Vestments, Roods, and Fonts aforesaid be likewise utterly defaced, Yt hereunto all persons within this Kingdome whom it may concerne are hereby required at their perill, to yield due obedience.

Provided that this Ordinance, or any thing therein contained, shall not extend to any Image, Picture or coat of Armes, in Glasse, Stone, or otherwise, in any Church, Chappell, Church-yard or place of publique Prayer as aforesaid, set up or graven onely for a monument of any King, Prince or Nobleman, or other dead person which hath not bin commonly reputed or taken for a Saint: But that all such Images, Pictures and Coats of Armes may stand and continue in like manner and forme as if this Ordinance had never bin made: And the severall Church-Wardens or

Overseers of the people of the said severall Churches and Chappels respectively, and the next adjoyning Justice of the Peace, or deputy Lieutenant, are hereby required to see the due performance hereof. And that the repairing of the Walles, Windows, Grounds, and other places which shall be broken, or impaired by any the meanes aforesaid, shall be done and performed by such person and persons, as are for the same end and purpose nominated and appointed by a former Ordinance of Parliament of the eight and twentieth of August, 16[4]3. For the utter demolishing of Monuments of superstition or Idolatry.

Samuel Pepys and John Evelyn

The Long Parliament theoretically continued in authority until 1660—though the real power was exercised by Oliver Cromwell—when it was dissolved upon the restoration of the monarchy and the coronation of Charles II as king of England. Charles had spent most of the previous fourteen years as an exile on the European continent and had developed a taste for the contemporary French and Italian styles of church music, which featured orchestral "symphonies" and accompaniments. Thus, when he returned to England, he reorganized the Chapel Royal to include instruments of the new violin family and music in the Continental style. Two famous English diarists of the seventeenth century, Samuel Pepys (1633-1703) and John Evelyn (1620-1706), both noted occasions when they attended Chapel Royal services featuring the new approach to church music. Pepys seems to have appreciated the change, but Evelyn was less sanguine about it.

From Samuel Pepys, Diary. *Diary and Correspondence of Samuel Pepys, Esq., F.R.S. from His MS. Cypher in the Pepysian Library*, deciphered by Mynors Bright. (New York: Dodd, Mead & Company, 1889), vol. 2, 331-332 (September 7, 1662).

7th. To White Hall Chappell, where I heard a good sermon of the Deane of Ely's, upon returning to the old ways, and a most excellent anthem, with symphonys between, sung by Captain Cooke. Home with Mr. Fox and his lady; and there dined with them.

September 14, 1662 (ibid., vol. 2, 335-336).

14th (Lord's day). By water to White Hall, by the way hearing that the Bishop of London had given a very strict order against boats going on Sundays, and as I came back again, we were examined by the masters of the company in another boat; but I told them who I was. To White Hall chapel, where sermon almost done, and I heard Captain Cooke's new musique. This is the first day of having vialls and other instruments to play a symphony between every verse of the anthem; but the musique more full than it was the last Sunday, and very fine it is. But yet I could discern Captain Cooke to overdo his part at singing, which I never did before. Thence up into the Queene's presence, and there saw the Queene again as I did last Sunday, and some fine ladies with her; but, my troth, not many. Thence to Sir G. Carteret's, and find him to have sprained his foot and is lame, but yet hath been at chappell, and my Lady much troubled for one of her daughters that is sick. I dined with them, and a very pretty lady, their kinswoman, with them. My joy is, that I think I have good hold on Sir George and Mr. Coventry.

From John Evelyn, Diary. *The Diary of John Evelyn*, ed. William Bray (Washington D.C., and London: M. Walter Dunne, 1901), vol. 1, 366.

21st December, 1662. One of his Majesty's chaplains preached; after which, instead of the ancient, grave, and solemn wind music accompanying the organ, was introduced a concert of twenty-four violins between every pause, after the French fantastical light way, better suiting a tavern, or playhouse, than a church. This was the first time of change, and now we no more heard the cornet which gave life to the organ; that instrument quite left off in which the English were so skillful. I dined at Mr. Povey's, where I talked with Cromer, a great musician.

Anonymous

The return of traditional Anglicanism at the Restoration led to a significant increase in the number of organs to be found in English churches. The use of organs now began to extend not only to cathedrals but to parish churches as well. Furthermore, defenses of organs and other musical instruments began appearing in print. These answered some of the theological objections to instruments that had been raised over the centuries, but the main argument was simply the "usefulness of the thing it self" (Towerson).

From anonymous, *An Apology for the Organs and Prayers Used in the Church of England, in Answer to Some Fanatical Reflections upon Bells and Crutches in a Letter from a Gentleman in the City to His Friend* (London: B. Griffin, 1692), [1]-[2].

Sir, when you last entertained me with your good Company, you were extreamly obliging, especially in asserting the Doctrines of the Church of *England* to be pure and Apostolick: and as I endeavoured to confirm you in that good Opinion, I was at the same time as industirously concerned, to abate your prejudice against some of her Ceremonies: and as I have justly admired your even Temper, moderate Spirit and sound Judgment, therefore cannot but think you will pardon my freedom if for once I commit a Trespass upon your Patience, and endeavour to confute your Error, and remove your indigested Notions. In our late Conference you appeared much for Union; but you were so squeasie and cropsick, that you needed to consult a Physician to clear your Stomach from Phlegm and Choler: I remember you seemed much disturbed at our *Bells* and *Crutches*, which if our Church would shake off, we should find you in a better disposition to imbrace her Communion. Sir, if you cannot digest that you call popish and profane noise of Bells in our Steeples, (since you can not but know they were appointed for no other end but the Calling the People together to worship God) you would do well to think of some other Instruments: I confess I apprehend it more decent than winding the Horn, blowing the Trumpet, or beating the Drum. Sir, my kindness for your Personal Virtues is exceeding great, and I would gladly imploy my utmost thoughts in contributing towards the satisfying your reasonable Scruples, had I a Key to unlock your *dark Metaphors*: and whereas you desire us to shake off our *Bells* and lay aside our *Crutches*, I hope you will first prove we wear them. As for the word *Shake*, it is more proper to be used to *Quakers*; but shaking of Bells I judge most applicable to Morrice-Dancers: and such you represent us to be by your blind and obscure Sayings. But before I proceed to discourse further upon this Topick, I must unfold your meaning; The Organs in our Churches which so highly offend your scrupulous Consciences, and bugbear you out of our Communion, sufficiently incite us to pity your Understandings, and to prevail with you to lay aside Pride, Prejudice, and a peevish Spirit. Can you upon Scripture Grounds warrant your departure from us? and why are you [t]hus transported with indignation against our Church-Discipline, when you may be justly censured amongst those furious Zealots, who, as St. *Paul* bears Record, had a Zeal, but not according to Knowledge, and since from Holy Scripture we have but this general Rule for the Discipline of the Church: That *all things be done decently and in order*, you ought to prove her injunctions incongruous to the one, or the other; or to assign some solid Reasons for such your unchristian Clamors: but if the Wisdom and Experience of our Spiritual Pastors have thought fit to praise God with the Organ, (an Instrument proper to raise our dull

Affections, and, if possible, to charm us into the deepest contemplations of Love and Adoration of that incomprehensible Being which was, and is, and shall be for ever: 'Tis acknowledged these are but faint and imperfect Emblems of that perpetual Harmony we shall ere long be heartily ingaged in, when Mortals must put on Immortality. But you will object, it is the Heart and not the Voice that renders this service acceptable to God: as the Heart of a Good man is filled with Secret Love, and warm'd with Internal Devotion; so the Voice at that instant is an outward manifestation of our hearty and exalted Affections to the Supream Goodness: and that Organical Sound, mingling with the Voice, becomes a further Instrument of praise by helping our bodily Infirmities, chearing our Spirits, quickning our Affections to a rejoycing in future Heavenly Hope.

Gabriel Towerson

Gabriel Towerson (ca. 1635-1697) was educated at Queen's College, Oxford, and in 1692 became rector of London's St. Andrew Undershaft parish church. When the church acquired an organ in 1696, Towerson preached a sermon of dedication, in the process acknowledging that the use of organs in Anglican parish churches was still controversial, but pointing out the positive features of the instrument for assisting in the church's music.

From Gabriel Towerson, *A Sermon Concerning Vocal and Instrumental Musick in the Church. As it was delivered in the parish church of St. Andrew Undershaft, upon the 31th of May, 1696, being Whit-Sunday, and the day wherein the organ there erected was first made use of* (London: for B. Aylmer, 1696), [5]-6, 24-28.

The Purpose of the ensuing Discourse is to satisfie the double business of this day; That which prompts you to reflect upon the Graces of that Spirit, which did as this day descend upon the Church; And that which prompts you to commemorate that, and all other the Blessings of God to it with Psalms, and Hymns, and Spiritual Songs: Whether they be such as mount up to Heaven on the alone wings of their own breath; Or whether they be such as are also advantagd to their ascent thither by the breath of Musical Instruments, and both conducted, and pushed on by it. And may that Spirit, by which these, and all other Religious Actions ought to be directed, so assist me in the handling of the Exhortations that are now before me, that I may both *my self* apprehend; and set *before you* the due importance of each of them, and approve them both to your Reason, and Affections. . . .

5. I have hitherto proceeded with very little disturbance, because there are not many, that are Enemies to that Musick, which hath been hitherto considered. But I must not expect to pass on so smoothly while I deliver my Opinion concerning that Singing, and making Melody, which is attended with that of Musical *Instruments*; Because though our *Foreign* Writers allow of Singing, even where the Composition is more Artificial, yet they represent Instrumental Musick among the Rudiments of the Law,[1] as long before them the *Authour* of the Questions and Answers *ad Orthodoxos*[2] as a thing *only suitable to that Infant-state, wherein those of the Law were. For which cause the use of it was* (as he saith) *taken away in the Churches, and simple Singing left in its stead.*

What reason there is to look upon *Instrumental* Musick as a Rudiment of the Law, I cannot understand; because throughout the whole *Law* there is no mention of any other Instrument, than of the Trumpet, and which too appears rather to have been used[3] to give *notice of a Festival*, or to *call the People together* to celebrate it, than any proper attendant of its service. And as little reason I think there is, why we should look upon such Instruments as accommodated only to an *Infant-state*, and particularly to that of the Law; Because as there is mention of the use of them before the giving of the Law, and particularly at the Singing of that so famous Song of *Moses* upon the overthrow of the *Egyptians* in the Red Sea: (For *Moses* tells us[4] that *Miriam* the Prophetess, and the Women that attended her, did not only answer that Song of his with their Mouths, but with their *Timbrels*); so it appears that they were mostly employ'd, if not also appointed, when the Spiritual part of Gods Worship was at the highest among that People, (as to be sure it was in the time of *David*) and frequent and earnest Exhortations[5] made to the Praising of God with them. For who can look upon that as a Legal Institution, which was the attendant of the most Spiritual Worship, which ever the *Jews* had, and which hath alwayes been thought so Spiritual, that the Scriptures of the *New Testament* call upon us to make use of it, and the Church of God hath from the beginning made the principal part of it's.

[1]*Calvin. Comment. in* Psalm 33.2. *& alibi.*

[2]*Resp. ad qu.* 107.

[3]Num. 10.2. Lev. 24.9.

[4]Exo. 15.20.

[5]Psalm 33.—81. 150. *& alibi passim.*

This I take to be a sufficient Answer to an Objection, that is without all ground; because that very *Law*, to which it entitles *Instrumental Musick*, makes no mention of it. But I will however, to silence, if possible, the Clamours of Unreasonable Men, make it appear to have a sufficient foundation in that *Reason* which is common to us all, and which as it had a being long before the *Law of Moses*, so will continue of force, as long as we our selves shall: That, I mean, which perswades the use of such things in the Worship of God, as may be *serviceable to it*, or *helpful to the Devotions* of those that have a part in it.

For whereas the greater part of those that assist at the Worship of God, neither have, nor can well be supposed to have, any such skill in Singing, as to carry them with any tolerable *concent* through the Psalms, or Hymns that are used in the Church; By which means the Service it self comes to be abhorred, or, at least, many, that are concerned in it, are forced to give it over: The *Organ*, in particular, both by the *Lowdness*, and the *Harmoniousness* thereof doth, with a kind of grateful Violence, carry the Voices of Men along with it, and not only prevents any such indecent Discords as might otherwise arise, but makes their Voices indeed and in truth to answer that Melody, which is here exhorted to, and is, it may be, the only *Instrument* that can with any certainty procure it.

Whereas again the Affections of the generality of Men are, and will be dull, but however there is none of us all, whose Affections do not often want quickening in the Worship of God; In which case Reason it self will perswade the use of such probable means as may be helpful to us in the stirring of them, but especially in that part of Gods Service, which requires a sprightly and a chearful Mind: What can be more reasonable than to make use of such *Instruments* of Musick, as tend in their own Nature to excite and improve them; yea, do not seldom transform Men into a perfectly different Temper from what they were before they listned to them?

So great reason is there to believe that *Instrumental* Musick, as well as *Vocal*, came into the Church, not from any perverse imitation of the *Law of Moses*, as some have fondly enough imagined, but from the apparent usefulness of the thing it self, and which Mens common Reason, as well as Experience, led them to the approbation of. If it came not in sooner, or did not spread more universally when it did, (for it appears not to have come into the Church till the Year 660,[6] nor to have diffused it self every where when it did) it was either because the disconsolateness

---

[6] *Joan. Bona* Divin. Psalmo. Cap. 17. Sect. 2.

of the Times did not comport with it, as to be sure those of the first Three Hundred Years did not; Or because Men had an unreasonable scruple against it as a thing only suited to the Infant-state of the Synagogue; Or, because, where it was received, it was not managed with that Gravity, wherewith all Ecclesiastical Offices ought to be attended. For against the thing, in it self considered, there can be no scruple at all; neither have there been more devout Men upon Earth, than those who have delighted in it, and practised it with signal advantage to themselves, if the Prophet *David*, and our Divine *Herbert* may pass for such.

What remains then, but that having in the first place endeavour'd to get our selves replenished with the *Spirit*, and particularly with those Graces of it, which serve more immediately to the exciting of a Spiritual and Heavenly Joy, we endeavour to keep it up, and improve, and express it by Psalms, and Hymns, and Spiritual Songs? Singing indeed, and making Melody *in our Heart to the Lord*, because without that it can be no Melody in the Ears of the Divine Majesty, but withal Singing, and making Melody with our Voices, and Instruments, as well as in our Hearts, because these do in their way express our grateful resentment of his Benefits, and do moreover excite, and improve that Melody of the Heart, which we have said to be so acceptable to him.

Part IV
The Eighteenth and Nineteenth Centuries

8
Instrumental Music in Roman Catholic Italy and France

THE use of the organ and other musical instruments had become common in Roman Catholic countries during the sixteenth and seventeenth centuries, but problems associated with them continued during the eighteenth and nineteenth centuries. As the writings in this chapter show, instrumentalists came under censure for the amount of time expended on their music, the manner in which they played their instruments, and the poor quality of some of the music that was performed.

Pope Benedict XIII

Some of the problems related to instruments among eighteenth- and nineteenth-century Roman Catholics are illustrated by the nuns of the convent of St. Radegundis in Milan, who, as the following document tells us, played orchestral instruments on which they introduced secular melodies (or secular styles?), spent their prayer time practicing, and became too familiar with musicians from outside the convent. These activities came to the attention of Pope Benedict XIII (1649-1730), who prohibited the nuns from playing instruments during divine service. The Pope's decree might have had the desired effect among the nuns of St. Radegundis, but the use of orchestral instruments continued to be common in Italian churches, even in Rome itself.

Pope Benedict XIII, Decree concerning the use of figured music and instruments by the nuns of St. Radegundis in Milan (1728). Translated by Robert F. Hayburn in *Papal Legislation on Sacred Music 95 A. D. to 1977 A. D.* (Collegeville, Minn.: Liturgical Press, 1979), 89-90.

Our Beloved Son, Julius Anesius, Abbot of the Monastery of S. Simplicianus of the City of Milan, has made known to Us lately, since he is the

President of the Cassinese Congregation of the Order of St. Benedict, that in the ancient Constitutions of the Monks of that Congregation, by order of Popes Leo X and Gregory XIII, Our predecessors, which they approved, that instrumental music and chant which are called "figured" were forbidden to them, and that scarcely ever is such music even now heard in the churches of this Congregation.

However, the nuns of the Convent of St. Radegundis of the City of Milan, nevertheless, with exceptional praise and enormous commendation of the monastic discipline of the Rule of St. Benedict, according to the rite and customs of the same Congregation, at the present time under the care and rule of the present Abbot, they profess adherence to the same. Yet at the same time some of these, to the neglect of the Gregorian Chant, which the monks of this Congregation accept as coming to them as a heritage from St. Gregory the Great, and others accept likewise, have departed from this norm for some years, and at the present time on feast days, and on the more solemn occasions. In such instances at Mass and at Vespers, they are accustomed to sing music of figured type, and to introduce, besides the organ, instruments of various types, which introduce secular melodies. Because of this practice, time is taken to learn this music, and whole days are taken away from prayer, to the detriment of the spiritual life of many of the nuns. Many of these are accustomed to prayer and recollection, but these practices impede the normal routine of the convent, take away the silence of recollection, and pious works are obstructed. As a result many pious souls are distracted and perturbed. But the worst part of the whole thing is that those nuns who are skilled in the art of music spend much time with persons of the same city speaking about the art of music, and the techniques of the same. Their superiors have forbidden this but all exhortations to the contrary are ignored. They have been told of the laws of Our predecessors of holy memory, Popes Innocent XI, and Clement XI, and of how these same Pontiffs have forbidden these same songs and symphonies under specific penalties and punishments.

But since as the same exposition is joined with long experience, a remedy for this manner of evil has been discovered, in order that it might be quickly removed. Thus, in order that this abuse might be cut at the very roots, and from which grave scandal is able to rise, as it is feared, the same must be checked as with an axe. The same Abbot Julius presiding well over the same, has made these known to Us, and desires that We should take means to rectify the above matter connected with the above-named nuns. These nuns have given themselves as offerings in the house of their Father, and have vowed themselves as spouses of Our Lord Jesus Christ. Some of them have consulted Abbot Julius, who is President of the Congregation, and with great fervor he has requested that these practices might be forbidden to each and every nun in the same convent. Thus for the present and for the future, and for each and every female who is to enter the convent of Saint Radegundis and for all living there now for the purpose of their education, with the permission of the Apostolic See, We set these rules concerning music. Never more, and at no time in the future may anyone for any reason, cause, or excuse make use of figured music, or dare to introduce musical instruments into the church and choir. Anyone who might do such a thing or dare to disobey this edict will suffer the punishment of interdict of the Church, under the disabilities and threats of excommunication *latae sententiae*. These same are reserved to Us personally, and to Our successors, with the exception of the moment of death when one may receive forgiveness. With this punishment goes likewise privation of active and passive voice to be heard, for those who go contrary to Our wishes. With Our Apostolic authority, and without any further declaration for the one who incurs this, We interdict and prohibit perpetually.

Given at Rome, from the Basilica of St. Mary Major, on the 19th of September, 1728.

Charles Burney

Charles Burney (1726-1814) was a prominent eighteenth-century English music teacher and composer, but is best known as the author of one of the first histories of music, *A General History of Music from the Earliest Ages to the Present Period* (1776-1789). In preparation for the writing of this volume, he took two extended trips to Europe, publishing the results of his observations of contemporary music in two volumes, *The Present State of Music in France and Italy* (1771) and *The Present State of Music in Germany, the Netherlands, and the United Provinces* (1773). In these volumes Burney often comments on sacred music, including some particularly interesting remarks on the use of instruments.

From Charles Burney, *The Present State of Music in France and Italy: or, The Journal of a Tour through Those Countries, Undertaken to Collect Materials for A General History of Music* (London: T. Becket and Co., 1771), 19-23 (Paris, June 14, 1770).

Thursday 14. This being *Féte Dieu*, or *Corpus Christi* Day, one of the greatest holidays in the whole year, I went to see the processions, and to hear high mass performed at Notre Dame. I had great difficulty to get thither. Coaches are not allowed to stir till all the processions, with which the whole town swarms, are over. The streets through which they are to pass in the way to the churches, are all lined with tapestry; or, for want of that, with bed curtains and old petticoats: I find the better sort of people, *(les gens comme il faut)* all go out of town on these days, to avoid the *embarras* of going to mass, or the *ennui* of staying at home. Whenever the host stops, which frequently happens, the priests sing a psalm, and all the people fall on their knees in the middle of the street, whether dirty or clean. I readily complied with this ceremony rather than give offence or become remarkable. Indeed, when I went out, I determined to do as other people did, in the streets and church, otherwise I had no business there; so that I found it incumbent on me to kneel down twenty times ere I reached Notre Dame. This I was the less hurt at, as I saw it quite general; and many much better dressed people than myself, almost prostrated themselves, while I only touched the ground with one knee. At length I reached the church, where I was likewise a *conformist*; though here I walked about frequently, as I saw others do, round the choir and in the great aisle. I made my remarks on the organ, organist, plain-chant, and motets. Though this was so great a festival, the organ accompanied the choir but little. The chief use made of it, was to play over the chant before it was sung, all through the Psalms. Upon enquiring of a young abbé, whom I took with me as a *nomenclator*, what this was called? *C'est proser*, 'Tis prosing, he said. And it should seem as if our word *prosing* came from this dull and heavy manner of recital. The organ is a good one, but when played full, the echo and reverberation were so strong, that it was all confusion; however, on the choir organ and echo stops I could hear every passage distinctly. The organist has a neat and judicious way of touching the instrument; but his passages were very old fashioned. Indeed what he played during the *offertorio*, which lasted six or eight minutes, seemed too stiff and regular for a voluntary. Several *motets*, or services, were performed by the choir, but accompanied oftener by the *serpent* than organ: though, at my first entrance into the French churches, I have frequently taken the *serpent* for an organ; but soon found it had in its effect something better and something worse than that instrument. These compositions are much in the way of our old church services, full of fugues and imitation; more contrivance and labour than melody. I am more and more convinced every day, that what I before observed concerning the adapting the English words to the old *canto fermo*, by Tallis, at the Reformation, is true; and it seems to me that music, in our cathedral service, was less reformed than any other part of the liturgy.

Venice, August 15, 1770 (ibid., 173-174).

Wednesday 15. I went this morning to St. Mark's church, at which, being a festival, the doge was present. I there heard high mass performed under the direction of Signor Galuppi, composer of the music. Upon this occasion there were six orchestras, two great ones in the galleries of the two principal organs, and four less, two on a side, in which there were likewise small organs. I was placed very advantageously in one of the great organ lofts, with Signor L'Atilla, assistant to Signor Galuppi.[1] The music, which was in general full and grave, had a great effect, though this church is not very happily formed for music, as it has five domes or cupolas, by which the sound is too much broken and reverberated before it reaches the ear.

Rome, November 18, 1770 (ibid., 373-378).

Sunday 18. I went this morning with Mr. Wyseman to the church of S. John Lateran[2]; it is the most antient church in Christendom. I here heard high mass performed in the Colonna chapel, by two choirs, and saw it played by Signor Colista, the celebrated organist of that church, on a little moveable organ. The music was by Signor Casali, Maestro di Capella, who was there to beat time. I was introduced both to him and to Signor Colista, after the service; and the latter upon being entreated to let me hear the great organ, very obligingly consented, upon condition that *Monsignore il Prefetto* of the church was applied to; which is a necessary ceremony in consequence of some injury formerly done to the instrument, by the malice or ignorance of a stranger who had played upon it. This

[1] This instrument has pedals, and but one row of box keys.

[2] Mr. Wyseman is a worthy English music-master, who is well known and esteemed by all the English at Rome, where he has so long been an inhabitant, that he has almost forgot his native tongue. He now lives in the *Palazzo Rafaele*, without the gates of Rome; where, during the first winter months, he has a concert every week till the operas begin. It was here that the great Raphael lived, where there are still some of his paintings in fresco; and where the late Duke of York, the Prince of Brunswick, and several other great personages, gave concerts to the first people of Rome.

application was readily undertaken, and the permission obtained, by Signor Casali.

I was conducted into the great organ-loft by Signor Colista, who did me the favour to open the case, and to shew me all the internal construction of this famous instrument. It is a thirty-two feet organ, and the largest in Rome. It was first built in 1549, and has undergone two repairs since; the one in 1600, by Luca Blasi Perugino; and a second, a few years since, under the direction of the present organist. It has thirty-six stops, two sets of keys, long eighths, an octave below double F. and goes up to E. in altissimo. It has likewise pedals; in the use of which Signor Colista is very dextrous. His manner of playing this instrument seems to be the true organ stile, though his taste is rather ancient; indeed the organ stile seems to be better preserved throughout Italy than it is with us; as the harpsichord is not sufficiently cultivated to encroach upon that instrument. Signor Colista played several fugues, in which the subjects were frequently introduced on the pedals, in a very masterly manner. But it seems as if every virtue in music was to border upon some vice; for this stile of playing precludes all grace, taste, and melody; while the light, airy harpsichord kind of playing, destroys the *sostenuto* and richness of harmony and contrivance of which the divine instrument is so peculiarly capable.

It is very extraordinary that the *swell*, which has been introduced into the English organ more than fifty years, and which is so capable of expression and of pleasing effects, that it may well be said to be the greatest and most important improvement that ever was made on any keyed instrument, should be still utterly unknown in Italy.[3] The *touch* too of the organ, which our builders have so much improved, still remains in its heavy, noisy state; and now I am on this subject, I must observe, that most of the organs I have met with on the Continent, seem to be inferior to ours built by father Smith, Byfield, or Snetzler, in every thing but size. As the churches there are often immense, so are the organs; the tone is indeed somewhat softened and refined by space and distance; but when heard near, it is intolerably coarse and noisy; and though the number of stops in these large instruments is very great, they afford but little variety,

[3]It is the same with the *Beat* upon the unison, octave, or any consonant sound to a note on the violin, which so well supplies the place of the old close-shake: for this beautiful effect, if not wholly unknown, is at least neglected by all the violin performers I heard on the continent, though so commonly and successfully practised in England by those of the Giardini school.

being, for the most part, duplicates in unisons and octaves to each other, such as the great and small 12ths, flutes, and 15ths: hence in our organs not only the touch and tone, but the imitative stops are greatly superior to those of any other organs I have met with.

Immediately after dinner I went to St. Peter's, where there was a great *Funzione* for the feast of it's foundation. The vespers were said by Cardinal York, assisted by several bishops: there were Mazzanti and Cristofero to sing, besides several other supernumeraries, and the whole choir. The fat Giovannini, famous for playing the violoncello, as well as for being one of the *maestri di capella* of St[.] Peter's, beat time. The solo parts were finely sung by the two singers just mentioned, and the chorusses by two choirs, and two organs, were admirably performed. Part of the music was by Palestrina, part by Benevoli, and the rest modern, but in a grave and majestic stile. I never heard church music, except that of the Pope's chapel, so well performed. There were no other instruments than the two organs, four violoncellos, and two double bases. Some fugues and imitations in dialogue between the two choirs were performed, which had a very fine effect. The service was in the large canonical, or winter chapel on the left, in which is the largest organ of St. Peter's church.[4]

Felix Mendelssohn

Felix Mendelssohn (1809-1847) was one of the great German composers of the nineteenth century. His aptitude for composition showed itself at an early age, particularly in the overture to Shakespeare's *A Midsummer Night's Dream,* written at the age of seventeen. Among his subsequent works, the best known are the *Songs Without Words* for piano; the Violin Concerto; the *Italian*, *Scottish*, and *Reformation* symphonies; and the oratorios *Elias* (Elijah) and *Paulus* (St. Paul). Mendelssohn is also highly regarded for the scope and quality of his letter writing. In 1830-1831 he made a trip to Italy at the suggestion of Goethe. During this trip he visited a Venetian church to view its art objects. In a letter to his former teacher, Carl Friedrich Zelter, Mendelssohn gave his impression of the organ playing he encountered on this visit.

From Felix Mendelssohn, Letter to Carl Friedrich Zelter (October 16, 1830). Translated by Lady [Grace] Wallace in Felix Mendelssohn Bartholdy, *Letters from Italy and Switzerland*, 9th ed. (London: Longmans, Green, 1887), 35-38.

---

[4]There are no other organs, nor indeed choirs at St. Peter's than those in the side chapels; so that the distance between the west door and the great altar, is wholly a free and unbroken space.

Dear Professor,
I have entered Italy at last, and I intend this letter to be the commencement of a regular series of reports, which I purpose transmitting to you, of all that appears to me particularly worthy of notice. Though I only now for the first time write to you, I must beg you to impute the blame to the state of constant excitement in which I lived, both in Munich and in Vienna. It was needless for me to describe to you the parties in Munich, which I attended every evening, and where I played the piano more unremittingly than I ever did in my life before; one *soirée* succeeding another so closely, that I really had not a moment to collect my thoughts. Moreover, it would not have particularly interested you, for after all, "good society which does not offer materials for the smallest epigram," is equally vapid in a letter. I hope that you have not taken amiss my long silence, and that I may expect a few lines from you, even if they contain nothing save that you are well and cheerful.

The aspect of the world at this moment is very bleak and stormy, and much that was thought durable and unchangeable, seems to fall to pieces in the course of a couple of days. It is then doubly welcome to hear well-known voices, to convince us that there are certain things which cannot be annihilated or demolished, but remain firm and steadfast; and as at this moment I am very uneasy at not having received any news from home for the last four weeks, and at finding no letters from my family, either at Trieste or here, so a few lines from you, written in your old fashion, would both cheer and gratify me, especially as they would prove that you think of me with the same kindness that you have always done from my childhood to the present time.

My family have no doubt told you of the exhilarating impressions made on me by the first sight of the plains of Italy. I hurry from one enjoyment to another hour by hour, and constantly see something novel and fresh; but immediately on my arrival I discovered some masterpieces of art, which I study with deep attention, and contemplate daily for a couple of hours at least. These are three pictures by Titian,—the "Presentation of Mary as a Child in the Temple;" the "Assumption of the Virgin;" and the "Entombment of Christ." There is also a portrait by Giorgione, representing a girl with a cithern in her hand, lost in thought, and looking forth from the picture in serious meditation (she is apparently about to begin a song, and you feel as if you must do the same): besides many others.

To see these alone would be worth a journey to Venice; for the fruitfulness, genius, and devotion of the great men who painted these pictures, seem to emanate from them afresh as often as you gaze at their works, and I do not much regret having scarcely heard any music here; for I suppose I must not venture to include the music of the angels, in the "Assumption," encircling Mary with joyous shouts of welcome; one beating the tambourine, a couple of others blowing away on strange crooked flutes, another lovely group singing—or the music floating in the thoughts of the cithern player. I have only once heard anything on the organ, and miserable it was. I was gazing at Titian's "Martyrdom of St. Peter" in the Franciscan Church. Divine service was going on, and nothing inspires me with more solemn awe than when on the very spot for which they were originally designed and painted, those ancient pictures in all their grandeur, gradually steal forth out of the darkness in which the long lapse of time has veiled them.

As I was earnestly contemplating the wondrous evening landscape with its trees, and angels among the boughs, the organ commenced. The first sound was quite in harmony with my feelings: but the second, third, and in fact all the rest, quickly roused me from my reveries, and restored me to my senses, for this is what the fellow was playing in church and during divine service, and in the presence of respectable people:

and the "Martyrdom of St. Peter" actually stood by his side! I was therefore in no great hurry to make the acquaintance of the organist. There is no regular Opera here at this moment, and the gondoliers no longer sing Tasso's stanzas; moreover, what I have hitherto seen of modern Venetian art, consists of poems framed and glazed on the subject of Titian's pictures, or Rinaldo and Armida, by a new Venetian painter, or a St. Cecilia by a ditto, besides various specimens of architecture in no style at all; as all these are totally insignificant, I cling to the ancient masters, and study how they worked. Often, in so doing, I have felt musically inclined, and have been composing industriously during my stay.

9
Instrumental Requirements in Germany and Austria

MARTIN Luther's generous attitude toward the use of musical instruments in worship ensured that organs and orchestras would find ready acceptance in the German Evangelical church. During the eighteenth century, the principal churches of the larger towns generally maintained an orchestra, whose chief task was to accompany the cantata or other music sung by the choir. Orchestral instruments were also common in the major churches of Roman Catholic Austria, where they were employed as accompaniment for the concert Mass. The two writings in this chapter detail some of the types of instruments that were desired and how they were distributed.

J. S. Bach

J. S. Bach (1685-1750), one of history's most remarkable composers, spent his life serving as musician at a number of German churches and minor courts. His longest tenure came as director of music for St. Thomas church and the town of Leipzig (1723-1750). In this position it was his responsibility to provide a cantata for nearly every Sunday of the year, in addition to other special occasions. These works were performed by the scholars of the *Thomasschule*, with occasional assistance by members of the town band or other local musicians. The admission of too many boys with little musical aptitude into the school led Bach to pen the following memorandum to his supervisors, the town council of Leipzig. This invaluable document not only reveals Bach's ideals for the performance of his cantatas and other works, but also what was actually available to him. The instrumental requirements should be particularly noted. Much the same dichotomy between musical expectations and actual availability of quality singers and instrumentalists was probably characteristic of many other German churches of the time.

J. S. Bach, "Brief, Yet Very Necessary Outline of a Well-Ordered Church Music; together with some random thoughts on the decline of the same" (1730). Werner Neumann and Hans-Joachim Schulze, eds., *Schriftstücke von der Hand Johann Sebastian Bachs*, vol. 1 of *Bach-Dokumente . . . Supplement zu Johann Sebastian Bach Neue Ausgabe Sämtliche Werke* (Kassel, Germany: Bärenreiter, 1963), 60-64.

For a well-ordered church music it is necessary to have vocalists and instrumentalists.

The vocalists in this place are drawn from the Thomas students, and are of four kinds, that is, sopranos, altos, tenors, and basses.

Now for the choruses of the church pieces to be arranged correctly, as is fitting, the vocalists must be divided further into 2 kinds, that is, concertists and ripienists.

Normally, there are 4 concertists; sometimes 5, 6, 7, or 8, if one would do music for multiple choirs.

The ripienists must also be at least eight in number, with two to a part.

The instrumentalists are also divided into different sorts, that is, violinists, oboists, flutists, trumpeters, and timpanists. NB. By violinists is also meant those who play violas, violoncellos, and bass viols.

The Thomas school students are 55 in number. These 55 are divided into 4 choirs for the 4 churches in which they must sing partly concerted music, partly motets, and partly chorales. In 3 of the churches—St. Thomas, St. Nicolai, and the New Church—the students must all be musical. The rest are placed in the Peter's Church, namely those who have little understanding of music and can scarcely sing even a chorale.

Each musical choir should have at least 3 sopranos, 3 altos, 3 tenors, and the same number of basses, so that, if perhaps one is indisposed (as very often happens, and especially at this time of year, as may be proved by the prescriptions that have been written by the school doctor), at least a 2-choir motet can be sung. (NB. It is even better when the group is set up so that there are 4 people to a part, and thus each choir can contain 16 persons.)

This makes the number of persons who must understand music 36 in all.

The instrumental music consists of the following parts, that is:

2 or even 3 for the	Violin 1.
2 or 3 for the	Violin 2.
2 for the	Viola 1.

2 for the	Viola 2.
2 for the	Violoncello.
1 for the	Bass viol.
2 or even, if conditions warrant, 3 for the	Oboe.
1 or even 2 for the	Bassoon.
3 for the	Trumpets.
1 for the	Timpani.

total 18 persons at least for the instrumental music. NB. If it happens that the church piece is also composed with flutes (which may be either recorders or transverse flutes), which very often happens for the sake of variety, at least 2 more persons are necessary. This makes 20 instrumentalists altogether.

The number of persons who are available for the church music is 8, that is, 4 town pipers, 3 professional violinists, and an apprentice. Of their abilities and musical knowledge, however, modesty forbids me to speak frankly. However, it should be cosidered that they are partly retired, partly also not in such practice as they ought to be.

The arrangement is as follows:

Mr. Reiche	1st Trumpet.
Mr. Genßmar	2nd Trumpet.
vacant	3rd Trumpet.
vacant	Timpani.
Mr. Rother	1st Violin.
Mr. Beyer	2nd Violin.
vacant	Viola.
vacant	Violoncello.
vacant	Bass viol.
Mr. Gleditsch	1st Oboe.
Mr. Kornagel	2nd Oboe.
vacant	3rd Oboe or Tenor.
The Apprentice	Bassoon.

Thus, the following people—who are very necessary, in part for reinforcement, in part for the parts that cannot be omitted—are missing, namely:

2 Violinists for the 1st Violin.
2 Violinists for the 2nd Violin.
2 that play the Viola.
2 Violoncellists.

1 Bass violist.

2 for the Flutes.

The deficiency that has been pointed out has until now had to be made up partly from the students, but mostly from the alumni. The students have been willing to do this in hopes that they might occasionally receive a reward, perhaps a stipend or honorarium (as was hitherto customary). However, this no longer happens; indeed, the few small favors that were formerly bestowed on the musical chorus have successively been entirely withdrawn, and with this has also been lost the cooperation of the students, for who will work or do service for nothing? Furthermore, it should be remembered that for lack of accomplished people, the 2nd Violin has mostly—and the Viola, Violoncello, and Bass viol always—had to be given to students, and it is easy to imagine what is thereby lost to the vocal choir. This has only touched upon the Sunday music. But should I mention the music for festival days (such as those in which music must be performed simultaneously in the two principal churches), the lack of the necessary personnel will be even more obvious, especially since I must supply to the other choir all the students who play one or another instrument and must make do without their assistance.

Furthermore, it cannot remain unmentioned that so many unfit and—for music—not very well qualified boys have been received up to now that the music must necessarily become inferior and unsuccessful. For it can be readily understood that a boy who knows very little of music, indeed, one who cannot even form a second in his throat, cannot have natural musicianship; consequently, he cannot be employed for music at all. And even those who do bring some of the principles with them to the school cannot be used right away, despite the demand. For time will not permit such first to train for years until they are skilful enough to be used, but as soon as they are received they are distributed to the choirs, where they must at least be able to keep the beat and pitch to be useful in the service. Now, when every year some of those who are musical leave the school and others who are not ready to be used or have no ability are substituted in their places, it is easy to conclude that the musical choir must be unsuccessful.

For it is notorious that my predecessors, Schell and Kuhnau, already had to rely on the assistance of the students when they wanted to produce a complete and melodious-sounding music. They were able to do this in part because in the past A Most Noble and Most Wise Council favored some vocalists with stipends—such as a bass, and a tenor, and even an alto—as well as instrumentalists—particularly 2 violinists—to the consequent strengthening of the church's musical life.

But now, since the state of music is completely different from the way it was before—the art having very much increased and the change of taste deserving of astonishment, so much so that our ears will no longer listen to the former kind of music, and considerably more assistance is needed in obtaining the right people to achieve the desired musical taste, perform the new kinds of music, and consequently be in the position of giving satisfaction to the composer and his works—the few favors formerly bestowed ought to have been increased rather than decreased and withdrawn completely from the musical choir. Indeed, it is quite remarkable that German musicians must be adept at many kinds of music, whether it comes from Italy or France, England or Poland, and do it extemporaneously like the virtuosos for whom it was written and who have studied it for a long time and almost know it by heart, and who besides receive good pay as a reward for their trouble and diligence; yet this is not taken into account, for they [German musicians] must take care of themselves and worry about their livelihood, and cannot think about improving, much less distinguishing, themselves. For an example that proves this assertion, one needs only to go to Dresden and see how His Royal Majesty's musicians are paid; it cannot be denied that when the musicians have to give no thought to their livelihood or to embarrassment regarding the same, and when each has to excell at only a single instrument, the result must be most excellent and wonderful to hear. The conclusion is, therefore, easily drawn, that the withdrawing of the favors has deprived me of the ability to put the music on a better footing.

In conclusion, I find it necessary to append the number of the current pupils and the musical progress of each, and then to leave for your fuller consideration whether satisfactory music can be expected in the future or whether greater decline is to be feared. However, it is necessary to divide the whole group into three categories. Those who are serviceable follow:

(1) Pezold, Lange, Stoll, *Prefects*. Frick, Krause, Kittler, Pohlreüter, Stein, Burckhard, Siegler, Nitzer, Reichhard, Krebs older and younger, Schönemann, Heder, and Dietel.

The motet singers, who must first show more improvement before they can participate in figural music, are as follows:

(2) Jänigke, Ludewig older and younger, Meißner, Neücke older and younger, Hillmeyer, Steidel, Heße, Haupt, Suppius, Segnitz, Thieme, Keller, Röder, Oßan, Berger, Lösch, Hauptman, and Sachse.

The last group is not very musical, and their names are:

(3) Bauer, Graß, Eberhard, Braune, Seyman, Tietze, Hebenstreit, Wintzer, Ößer, Leppert, Haußius, Feller, Crell, Zeymer, Guffer, Eichel, and Zwicker.

Total: 17 serviceable, 20 not yet serviceable, and 17 unfit. Leipzig, the 23rd of Aug. 1730.

Joh. Seb. Bach
Director of Music

Wolfgang Amadeus Mozart

Wolfgang Amadeus Mozart (1756-1791) was one of the three great Austrian composers of the Classical period, the others being Franz Joseph Haydn and Ludwig van Beethoven. Unlike J. S. Bach, Mozart spent most of his short life in employment outside the church. Nevertheless, he composed a considerable amount of church music, including orchestrally accompanied Masses and "church sonatas," multi-movement pieces for small orchestra—usually two violins and bass—and organ that were intended to be performed between the Epistle and Gospel lessons in the Mass (thus, they are also sometimes called "Epistle sonatas"). The following letters from Mozart to his friend Padre Martini and to his father reveal some of the instrumental expectations for Roman Catholic concerted sacred music in late-eighteenth-century Salzburg and Mannheim.

Letter to Padre Martini, September 4, 1776. Translated by Lady [Grace] Wallace in *The Letters of Wolfgang Amadeus Mozart (1769-1791)*, 2 vols. (New York: Hurd and Houghton, 1866), 53-54. Quotation marks around the original translation have been omitted.

Salzburg, Sept. 4, 1776.

Most Reverend and Esteemed Father and Maestro,—

The veneration, the esteem, and the respect I feel for your illustrious person, induce me to intrude on you with this letter, and also to send you a small portion of my music, which I venture to submit to your masterly judgment. Last year, at Monaco, in Bavaria, I wrote an opera buffa ("La finta Giardiniera") for the Carnival. A few days previous to my departure from thence, his Electoral Highness wished to hear some of my contrapuntal music; I was therefore obliged to write this motett in haste, to allow time for the score to be copied for his Highness, and to arrange the parts so that it might be produced on the following Sunday at grand mass at the offertory. Most dear and highly esteemed Maestro, I do entreat you to give me unreservedly your candid opinion of the motett. We live in this world in order always to learn industriously, and to enlighten each other by means of discussion, and to strive vigorously to promote the progress of science and the fine arts. Oh, how many and many a time have I desired to be nearer you, that I might converse and discuss with your Reverence! I live in a country where music has very little success, though, exclusive of those who have forsaken us, we have still admirable professors, and more particularly composers of great solidity, knowledge, and taste. We are rather badly off at the theatre from the want of actors. We have no *musici*, nor shall we find it very easy to get any, because they insist upon being well paid; and generosity is not a failing of ours. I amuse myself in the mean time by writing church and chamber music; and we have two excellent contrapuntists here, Haydn and Adlgasser. My father is maestro at the Metropolitan church, which gives me an opportunity to write for the church as much as I please. Moreover, my father has been thirty-six years in the service of this court, and knowing that our present Archbishop neither can nor will endure the sight of elderly people, he does not take it to heart, but devotes himself to literature, which was always his favorite pursuit. Our church music is rather different from that of Italy, and the more so, as a mass including the *Kyrie*, *Gloria*, *Credo*, the *Sonata all' Epistola*, the *Offertory* or *Motett*, *Sanctus*, and *Agnus Dei*, and even a solemn mass, when the Prince himself officiates, must never last more than three-quarters of an hour. A particular course of study is required for this class of composition. And what must such a mass be, scored with all the instruments, war-drums, cymbals, &c., &c.! Oh! why are we so far apart, dearest Signor Maestro? for how many things I have to say to you! I devoutly revere all the Signori *Filarmonici*. I venture to recommend myself to your good opinion; I shall never cease regretting being so distant from the person in the world whom I most love, venerate, and esteem. I beg to subscribe myself, reverend Father, always your most humble and devoted servant,

Wolfgang Amadeus Mozart.

From letter to his father, Mannheim, November 4, 1777 (ibid., 107-109).

I must now tell you about the music here. On Saturday, All-Saints' day, I attended high mass. The orchestra is very good and numerous. On each side ten or eleven violins, four tenors, two hautboys, two flutes, and two clarionets, two corni, four violoncellos, four bassoons, and four double basses, besides trumpets and kettle-drums. This should give fine music, but I would not venture to produce one of my masses here. Why? From their being short? No, everything is liked short. From their church style? By no means; but solely because *now* in Mannheim, under present circumstances, it is necessary to write chiefly for the instruments, for nothing can possibly be conceived worse than the voices here. Six soprani, six alti, six tenori, and six bassi, to twenty violins and twelve bassi, are in the same proportion as 0 to 1. Is it not so, Herr Bullinger? It proceeds from this:—The Italians are miserably represented: they have only two *musici* here, and they are already old. This race is dying out. These soprano singers, too, would prefer singing countertenor; for they can no longer take the high notes. The few boys they have are wretched. The tenor and bass just like our singers at funerals. Vogler, who lately conducted the mass, is barren and frivolous—a man who imagines he can do a great deal, and does very little. The whole orchestra dislike him. To-day, Sunday, I heard a mass of Holzbauer's, which is now twenty-six years old, but excellent. He writes very well, and has a good church style, arranges the vocal parts as well as the instrumental, and writes good fugues. They have two organists here; it would be worth while to come to Mannheim on purpose to hear them—which I had a famous opportunity of doing, as it is the custom here for the organist to play during the whole of the Benedictus. I heard the second organist first, and then the other. In my opinion the second is preferable to the first; for when I heard the former, I asked, "Who is that playing on the organ?" "Our second organist." "He plays miserably." When the other began, I said, "Who may that be?" "Our first organist." "Why, he plays more miserably still." I believe if they were pounded together, something even worse would be the result. It is enough to kill one with laughing to look at these gentlemen. The second at the organ is like a child trying to lift a millstone. You can see his anguish in his face. The first wears spectacles. I stood beside him at the organ and watched him with the intention of learning something from him; at each note he lifts his hands entirely off the keys. What he believes to be his *forte* is to play in six parts, but he mostly makes fifths and octaves. He often chooses to dispense altogether with his right hand when there is not the slightest need to do so, and plays with the left alone; in short, he fancies that he can do as he will, and that he is a thorough master of his organ.

From letter to his father, Mannheim, November 13, 1777 (ibid., 118-119).

The sonata for Madlle. Rosa Cannabich is finished. Last Sunday I played the organ in the chapel for my amusement. I came in while the *Kyrie* was going on, played the last part, and when the priest intoned the *Gloria* I made a cadence, so different, however, from what is usually heard here, that every one looked round in surprise, and above all Holzbauer. He said to me, "If I had known you were coming, I would have put out another mass for you." "Oh!" said I, "to puzzle me, I suppose?" Old Toeschi and Wendling stood all the time close beside me. I gave them enough to laugh at. Every now and then came a *pizzicato*, when I rattled the keys well; I was in my best humor. Instead of the *Benedictus* here, there is always a voluntary, so I took the ideas of the *Sanctus* and worked them out in a fugue. There they all stood making faces. At the close, after *Ita missa est*, I played a fugue. Their pedal is different from ours, which at first rather puzzled me, but I soon got used to it. I must now conclude. Pray write to us still at Mannheim.

10
The Bass Viol and Gallery Orchestra in England and America

As noted in chapter seven, some English parish churches began installing organs after the Restoration of the monarchy. However, these were mostly urban churches. Country parish churches seldom had the financial resources—or in some cases, the desire—to install such an instrument. Nevertheless, a number of these churches included members who played orchestral-type instruments. These instrumentalists sometimes banded together to form a "gallery orchestra," so named because they were gathered in the west gallery (balcony) of the church. In most instances, the gallery orchestra seems to have existed mainly to accompany the church's psalm singing and/or choir, not to provide independent instrumental music. The same phenomenon appeared in the early nineteenth century in American churches.

John Arnold

John Arnold (ca. 1715-1792) was a teacher of singing schools, parish clerk, and sometime organist in Great Warley, Essex. His most significant publication was *The Compleat Psalmodist* (1741 and later editions), a work to be used by country choirs. In the preface to the seventh edition, Arnold noted the increasing popularity of both the organ and orchestral instruments in country parish churches and observed that he had provided for the use of these in his book.

John Arnold, Preface to *The Complete Psalmodist: or the Organist's Parish-Clerk's, and Psalm-Singer's Companion*, 7th ed. (London: G. Bigg, 1779), [iii]-iv.

Singing of Psalms is so fit a Part of Divine Service, so natural an Expression of our Joy, and serves to so many noble Ends, that it comes recommended to us by the Practice of all Nations, seems to be as ancient as Public Worship, and has had the good Fortune to be approved of by all Parties of what Denomination soever; and therefore the Psalmist directs his Precept, not to any peculiar Church of GOD, but to all Lands, to serve the Lord with Gladness, and to come before his Presence with a Song.

Therefore the Design of this Undertaking is to better and improve this excellent and useful Part of our Service, to keep up an Uniformity in our Parish Churches, and bring them as much as may be to imitate their Mother Churches, the Cathedrals; so that all the Tunes in this Work are composed as near as can be after the Cathedral Manner, and so well adapted to the Compass of the several Voices, that all who are capable of Harmony, may join in this heavenly Chorus, and "Young Men and Maidens, old Men and Children, may praise the Name of the Lord; Psalm CXLVIII. Ver. 12." This will be a Means to add to the Church daily, and also make us glad to go into the House of the Lord; it will ravish our Hearts with the Harmony of God's Love and Goodness, whilst our Voices are joined in his Praises; that, having perfectly learned our Parts here, we may at last come to join with the Heavenly Chorus, and sing Hallelujahs to all Eternity.

In Order, to which End I have here presented you first with a complete and concise Introduction to Psalmody and musical Dictionary, and have selected five and thirty choice and capital Anthems, all set in Score, the greatest Part of them being composed by some of the most eminent Doctors and Masters of Music, Organists to several of our Cathedrals, at which Places they are now frequently performed; also by several other principal Choirs in England, and have collected near one Hundred of the very best Psalm Tunes, both ancient and modern, which I have properly adapted to the most sublime Portions of the Psalms; to which I have added a Set of Divine Hymns, suited to the Feasts and Fasts of the Church of England; with several excellent Canons of three and four Parts in one; proper to be sung after divine Service, whilst the Congregation is going out of Church, in lieu of a full Organ Voluntary, which is always performed in those Churches that are furnished with an Organ, to play the Congregation out, as it is stiled.

In this Edition, I have in the following Anthems and Psalm Tunes set the three upper Parts in the G Cliff, as I find it more eligible for country Choirs than the C Cliff; and since of late Years several Kinds of musical treble Instruments have been introduced into many country Churches, to accompany the Voices, as Violins, Hautboys, Clarinets, Vauxhumanes, &c. which Cliff is also much more suitable to those Instruments, and have placed the Tenor, which has the principal Air, and is designed for the leading Part, next the Bass, which also renders it much more convenient for Performers on the Organ, &c. and have also figured the Basses for the Organ, which, I flatter myself will make the whole Work of great Use to Organists, as well Parish Clerks as all Teachers and Scholars, and all other Lovers and Practicers of Divine Music whatever, and be the completest of the Kind and Price ever published.

I am not so vain as to flatter myself that this Collection is completely perfect: notwithstanding upon a judicious Probation, considering the largeness of the Untertaking, I hope the Errata will be found but small, having been careful to have it as correct as in my Power.

Every Man is pleased with his own Conceptions, but it is an impossibility for any Author to deliver that which will please all; but, since so large a Number as Two Thousand Copies of this Work is printed, each Edition, will, I presume, thoroughly evince the Usefulness thereof; and by the great Improvements and Additions which I have now made, I hope this Edition will be as candidly received as the former, and, if by what I now offer to the Public, continues to be instrumental, in propogating the Knowledge of this most excellent Art, of which I profess myself a very great Lover, it will give me ample Satisfaction, and with a secret Complaisance of Mind, I shall reflect on what I have done, to advance the Praise and Glory of that God, who is the Author of Harmony.

Let ev'ry Church give God what Churches owe,
Sending up Hallelujahs from below.

Great Warley, Essex,
July 19th 1779.
J. A.

John Byng

For evidence of the actual use of gallery orchestras in English parish churches, we may turn to the travel journals of John Byng (1743-1813). Byng received a commission in the British Army in 1760, serving for twenty years, after which he took a position in the Inland Revenue in Somerset, and subsequently became the fifth Viscount Torrington. During his service in the Inland Revenue, he undertook a series of "tours" to various locations in England and Wales, keeping a diary of persons and places he encountered. He paid special attention to church buildings, including both cathedrals and parishes, and often seems to have inquired about or observed the music to be heard in these buildings. The diary entries quoted in the following describe the use of a "gallery orchestra" in village parish churches that evidently contained no organ.

These were just the sorts of churches for which John Arnold had published his *Complete Psalmodist.*

From John Byng, *The Torrington Diaries*, ed. C. Bruyn Andrews (London: Eyre & Spottiswoode, 1934-1938), vol. 4, 139-140 (Thurgarton, Monday, June 8, 1789).

In regard to the Decay of religious Duties, which every person can remark, The Clerk said (to my regular Enquiry) that Singing had been disused about Six years.—At Botesford, yesterday I made the same enquiry, and found that tho the Psalmody there was on the decline, yet was it tolerably supported by 2 Bassoons, a Clarinet, and a german Flute.—Nothing shou'd be more encouraged as drawing both Young and Old to Church, than Church Melody, tho' the Profligacy and Refinement of the age has abandon'd and ridiculed it: But were I a Squire of a country Village I wou'd offer such Premiums and Encouragement, (of little cost to myself) as wou'd quickly rear an ambitious, and laudable desire of Psalm-Singing, and put forth a little Chorus of Children; than which nothing is more Elevating and Grateful and Sublime, hearing Innocence exert their little Voices in praise of their Creator.

For let Fashion say what it can, Every Ear is more gratified by a chorus of youth, than by the most violent Exertions of Taste.

Eaton, Sunday, June 19, 1791 (ibid., vol. 2, 316-317).

I was known, and well receiv'd at the Cock at Eaton, where before me was instantly serv'd a roasted shoulder of veal, and a dish of peas; I love an instant dinner, tho' I cannot say that I now know the feel of hunger! Another reason of my present haste was a resolution to go to evening service; (to pray for better weather, and a healthy pleasant tour;) so I summon'd in old Mrs W— for a conversation after dinner, and then with her, young Mrs W— and her children, devoutly march'd into the church; which is large, and handsome; and has been adorn'd with much stain'd glass.—The psalm singing, in a singing gallery, was tolerable, accompany'd by a flute and a hautboy: but such a reader, and preacher, as Mr Ls I hope is not often heard; tho' I fear so!

Folkingham, Sunday, June 26, 1791 (ibid., vol. 2, 337-338).

As tedious a morning to me, as to any other, idle, country lad, who wishes for the hour of eating, and then for the hour of sleeping. The

London newspapers came in at one o'clock, just before dinner time, when I ate of the family preparation, boil'd fowls, rst beef and young potatoes; which all travellers should certainly do, particularly on a Sunday.—My landlord then came in, 'fearing I was lonesome'; he now gets familiar, and will soon put his paws upon my lap; he prated away 'About the Duke of *Orlines*'s coming in here from hunting; whom he knew to be a foreigner by his earings, that he gave 9 guineas for a chaise to Grantham, 12 miles, and 10s. 6d. to the boys;' that *the High Chancellor* was also here, last year, and ask'd him 'If they grew good wheat hereabouts.' There would have been no end of my landlords jaw, had not the bells rang for church, to which I repair'd with my landlord, and landlady; (this I may call my religious tour, tho' I sadly fear that curiosity oft'ner than devotion leads me to church); he, fat, large, black, and shock-headed, in new bluff and blue; she, very like Mrs Hall in a brown silk.—Here were a numerous, and decent congregation, with a singing loft crouded; and amongst them one lady in a blue silk bonnet, who sung *notably*; but the bassoons, and hautboys, were too loud and shreiking: as for the clergyman, he went off in a loud, unintelligible key, like a lawyer reading deeds, and was truly intolerable. Had I been in the company of those I knew, I could not have refrain'd from laughter.—Much singing before the service; likewise the Magnificat, and two psalms: during the sermon mine host slept, and I slumber'd.

Middleham, Sunday, June 10, 1792 (ibid., vol. 3, 57-58).

Old White Rose; but then we old men, must think of the eleven days; for this new stile has perplexed us like a clock set forward: and no white, or red, roses will yet appear in the north.—When I went to bed last night I found my bed unusually heavy, and discovered that the blankets were doubled and that, so, I laid under four; which occasion'd a long fatigue of new making. I arose at 8 o'clock; (now this has been a shockingly late hour in a sultry summer's morn) and took another round of the Castle, whilst my coffee was preparing: at eleven o'cloclk I was attended to the Church, and became there an object of speculation, I suppose, as a stranger, and being put into the Dean's pew, (The Dean of Middleham). There was a decent, well-dressed, well-behaved congregation; with a singing-loft, from which there was too much singing from, about, a dozen voices, male, and female; and two bassoons, of better accompaniment than an organ: one of their attempts was too powerful for them,

'*And the Trumpet shall sound*', the bassoons imitating the trumpet. The service lasted long, but our service is much too long; The *Curate, the deputy* of *Mr Dean*, had a good voice, and perform'd tolerably.

William Bentley

William Bentley (1759-1819), a pioneer New England Unitarian, graduated from Harvard in 1777, and became pastor of the East Church in Salem, Massachusetts, in 1783, where he served for thirty-six years. Bentley maintained a diary from 1784 until his death. Scattered among the other items in the journal are several entries relating to the development and use of gallery orchestras in American churches, including his own.

William Bentley, Diary. Source: *The Diary of William Bentley, D. D.* (Gloucester, Mass.: Peter Smith, 1962), vol. 1, 418 (December 25, 1792).

25. For the first time in this place the Clarionet, & violin, introduced into Church Music. There is now no ground of complaint against the catholics.

October 28, 1795 (ibid., vol. 2, 163).

28. Sent & purchased at Boston a Bass Viol for 21 dollars. The fondness for Instrumental music in Churches so increases, that the inclination is not to be resisted. I have applied to M[r] Gardner to assist the Counter with his German Flute.

March 16, 1796 (ibid., vol. 2, 175).

16. The Violin for the first time was introduced last Sunday. We expect two German flutes, & a Tenor-Viol in addition to our present Bass viol.

September 15, 1797 (ibid., vol. 2, 239-240).

15. Sunday. Notes. John Watson & Wife & ch., death of his Mother Watson, pr. absent friends. Wid. Mary Gardner, d. of her Sister Watson. Martha Chard, d. of her husband abroad, pr. for Sons at Sea. Thomas Palfrey & Wife, d. of his Father, pr. for Brethren at Sea. James Very & Wife, d. of her Father Palfrey, pr. for Brother at Sea. Singing failing,

only the master at the Tenour & a man at the Bass Viol. The Ladies yet attend.

November 30, 1797 (ibid., vol. 2, 247-248).

30. The Day of public Thanksgiving, clear, cold, & very windy. We had for the first time a band of instruments in our Choir. The members were from different parts of the Town & were kind enough to give us the first exhibition they have ever made in public & the first of the kind ever on a public religious solemnity in the Town. The scandalous indifference to vocal music has obliged us to have recourse to such expedients or our Church music must have been lost. In all our societies the Bass viol has been used, having been introduced about two years since. A Violin & Clarionet followed in our worship. The number of these, with the Tenour viol, formed our Band on this solemnity. The order of service was, An air—Hymn 73, the instruments going over the tune, before the vocal music joined—Introductory prayer—An air—Lesson—Hymn 4—Prayer—32 Psalm—Sermon—Collection for the Poor, an air, with a chorus—Prayer—42 Hymn—Blessing—Concluding air.

January 1, 1805 (ibid., vol. 3, 131-132). The "Mr. Holyoke" referred to below was the early American composer Samuel Holyoke. The "Ship" was a tavern.

January 1. This day was appropriated for the dedication of the New South Meeting House at Salem. A large Band of music was provided & Mr. Holyoke took the direction. A double bass, 5 bass viols, 5 violins, 2 Clarionets, 2 Bassoons & 5 german flutes composed the Instrumental music. About 80 singers, the greater part males, composed the vocal music. It could not have the refinement of taste as few of the singers ever were together before & most were instructed by different masters. But in these circumstances it was good. The House was crowded & not half that went were accomodated. Mr. Hopkins, the Pastor, performed the religious service of prayer & preaching, & a Mr. Emerson of Beverly made the last prayer. The music had an excellent dinner provided for them at the Ship & the 16 ministers present dined in elegant taste at Hon. Jno. Norris Esqr. the principal character in the list of the Proprietors of the new Meeting House.

November 27, 1806 (ibid., vol. 3, 264-265).

27. Thanksgiving in N. H. Mass. Conn. & R. I. In Vermont next week. From the lowry weather, assembly not large & the Contribution 30D less than on last Thanksgiving day. Much of this loss we feel in Capt. B. Hodges. The foul weather prevented much of the folly of the meaner class & prevented much of the excitement to intemperance. In our Music we were assisted by Mr. Hart on the Claronet & some other persons whom I received at my house but who refused any pecuniary reward for their services. Contribution ab[out] 125D.

May 21, 1809 (ibid., vol. 3, 434).

The Baptist Itinerant who disturbed the Singers at the Brick Baptist Meeting a few Sundays since, was the man who is offered as a Teacher to youth and some of our daughters are to be sent into his family. Warned. They were playing & singing to the Bass Viol before service began & were reprimanded.

11
The Introduction of the Organ into American Churches

THE earliest organs to be used for religious services in what is now the United States were brought from Europe and placed in missions throughout the Spanish colonies during the sixteenth and seventeenth centuries. In the New England colonies, Puritan objections kept instruments out of Congregational and Independent churches until late in the eighteenth century. Of course, no such scruples affected the Anglicans or settlers from parts of Europe that were not under the influence of the Genevan Reformed tradition. Thus, it is not surprising that the more cosmopolitan city of Philadelphia seems to have boasted the most significant activity in this regard during the eighteenth century. This was due in part to the large number of German pietists who settled in Pennsylvania during the late seventeenth and early eighteenth centuries.

Justus Falckner

Justus Falckner (1672-1723) was born in Saxony, attended the University of Halle, and in 1700 immigrated to America. In 1702 he sent a letter to Heinrich Muhlen of Germany, pointing out how effective an organ would be in evangelizing the Indians and retaining youthful church members. Two years after this letter was written, Falckner was ordained to the Lutheran ministry in the Gloria Dei church of Philadelphia. The service was accompanied by instrumental music provided by an organist named Jonas and several members of the "Hermits of the Wissahickon" (a group of German pietistic mystics that in 1694 had immigrated to America under the leadership of Johannes Kelpius) playing the viol, oboe, trumpets, and timpani. Falckner's role, if any, in securing the organ for this service is not known.

From Justus Falckner, *Imprint of a Missive to Tit: Lord D. Henr. Muhlen, from Germanton in the American Province of Pennsylvania, otherwise New Sweden, the first of August, in the year of our salvation One thousand, seven hundred and one concerning the condition of the churches in America* (1702). Translated in Julius Friedrich Sachse, *Justus Falckner: Mystic and Scholar, Devout Pietist in Germany, Hermit on the Wissahickon, Missionary on the Hudson* (Philadelphia: for the author, 1903), 44-46. The quotation marks given around the original translation have been omitted; the German terms in parentheses are given as in Sachse.

I will here take occasion to mention that many others besides myself, who know the ways of this land, maintain that music would contribute much towards a good Christian service. It would not only attract and civilize the wild Indian, but it would do much good in spreading the Gospel truths among the sects and others by attracting them. Instrumental music is especially serviceable here. Thus a well-sounding organ would perhaps prove of great profit, to say nothing of the fact that the Indians would come running from far and near to listen to such unknown melody, and upon that account might become willing to accept our language and teaching, and remain with people who had such agreeable things; for they are said to come ever so far to listen to one who plays even upon a reed-pipe (*rohrpfeiffe*): such an extraordinary love have they for any melodious and ringing sound. Now as the melancholy, Saturnine stingy Quaker spirit has abolished (*relegiret*) all such music, it would indeed be a novelty here, and tend to attract many of the young people away from the Quakers and sects to attend services where such music was found, even against the wishes of their parents. This would afford a good opportunity to show them the truth and their error.

If such an organ-instrument (*Orgel-werck*) were placed in the Swedish church, (for the Germans as yet have no church, and the Swedish church is of a high build and resonant structure) it would prove of great service to this church. As the majority of the Swedes are young people, and mostly live scattered in the forest, far from the churches, and as we by nature are all inclined to good, and above all to what may serve our souls, such as the Word of God which is dead and gone, so are especially the youth; and it is so with the Swedish youth now under consideration. When they have performed heavy labor for the whole week, as is customary here, they would sooner rest on a Sunday, and seek some pleasure, rather than perhaps go several miles to listen to a sermon. But if there were such music there, they would consider church-going as a recreation for their senses.

Thus does Luther of blessed memory in one place highly recommend the use of the organ and sacred music for this very reason, that it is serviceable, and induces young and simple and, says he foolish folk, to listen unto and receive God's Word. It would also prove an agreeable thing for God, angels and men; if in this solitude and wilderness, which as it were struggles under so many *Secula*, the Lord of Hosts, with whom there is fulness of joy and at whose right hand there are pleasures for evermore, would be praised and honored with cymbal and organ, as he hath commanded. And it may be assumed that even a small organ-instrument and music in this place would be acceptable to God, and prove far more useful than many hundreds in Europe, where there is already a superfluity of such things; and the more common they are, the more they are misused.

If now Your Magnificence were kindly to intercede with his Serene Highness and Her Highness his Consort, and also with such other exalted personages with whom you are held in high esteem, and present to them the benefit to be hoped for; I doubt not, but that something could be effected. There are in Europe masters enough who build such instruments, and a fine one can be secured for 300 or 400 thalers. Then if an experienced organist and musician could be found, and a curious one who would undertake so far a journey, he would be very welcome here. In case this could not be, if we only had an organ, some one or other might be found here who had knowledge thereof.

Anonymous

In 1763 an anonymous Philadelphia author issued a pamphlet on *The Lawfulness, Excellency, and Advantage of Instrumental Musick in the Publick Worship of God.* The self-proclaimed goal of the work was to encourage Presbyterians and Baptists to reconsider their objections to instruments. On the title page and at several other points in the pamphlet, the author notes that he or she is a member of the Presbyterian church. The tract seems to have sold well, for a second edition was published in the same year. In the earlier part of the pamphlet, the author justifies the use of musical instruments largely by reference to the Old Testament. In the extract quoted below, the writer suggests that those who are opposed to the use of the organ in worship will change their minds if they will only listen without prejudice to a service at which one is played—presumably—well.

From anonymous, *The Lawfulness, Excellency, and Advantage of Instrumental Musick in the Publick Worship of God urg'd and enforc'd, from Scripture, and the example of the far greater part of Christians in all ages. Address'd to all (particularly the* Presbyterians *and* Baptists*) who have hitherto been taught to look upon the use of instrumental musick in the worship of God as unlawful. By a Presbyterian* (Philadelphia: William Dunlap, 1763), 26-31.

And I am well aware, that the far greater Part of those who decry the Use of Instrumental Musick in the Worship of God, have never had a single Opportunity even of being present at those Acts of Devotion in which the *Organ* is used, and of making the Experiment: And, because instrumental Jargon, *viz.* the Fiddle and Bagpipe, which they have all been bless'd in hearing,[1] (but which indeed have hardly any Resemblance at all of the Instrument I am contending for, *viz.* the *Organ*) are used in those riotous Assemblies that are calculated to excite carnal Mirth and Wantonness, they conclude, unheard, *all Instrumental Musick* must have a like Tendency to inflame the Passions to Sensuality.—With the same Force of Reason, Persons who are blinded with Prejudice and Ignorance, may cavil at and decry the Utility of the most useful Creatures and Inventions that God has appointed for the Support and Conveniency of Man:—Because Food and Raiment are frequently perverted to Voluptuousness and Wantonness, is it criminal to use either?—Because the richest Genius, like the most fertile Soil, when misled by a wrong Bent of Education, shoots up into the rankest Weeds, and instead of Vines and Olives, produces to its Possessor the most abundant Crop of Poison; are we therefore to suffer our Minds to remain in the darkest Ignorance?

This most disingenious Way of arguing, which is really the Foundation of *all that can be said* against the Use of Instrumental Musick in the Worship of God, is so very ridiculous, that one would wonder with what Face or Colour of Reason the Professors of Christianity, who have been bless'd with the Light of the Gospel, and who, if properly informed, might know better, could make Use of it.

Were not Advice thrown away on such, one would recommend it to them, laying Prejudice aside, to step into St. *Paul*'s in this City, or any other Church that has an Organ in it, and let them afterwards speak their Sentiments impartially:—They will find it impossible to be present at such Acts of Worship, without being elevated with the *divine Melody*, and feeling some Degree of that *heavenly Enthusiasm* which spreads itself through the whole Assembly; which is not only a strong Proof of

[1]This remark is more immediately intended for the Country, where it is well known Bigotry and certain narrow-contracted Notions, in Matters of Religion, reign most predominant.

the Propriety and Expediency of the Institution, but gives a pleasing Idea, that the Cause of Christianity in such Churches is not so desperate as the frantick Triumphs of the Vicious and Profane insinuate, or the Gloomy and Desponding are apt to believe.

I mention this Church in particular, as being the only *English* Congregation in the Province that has an Organ in it as yet, and as being a Church in which it will be confess'd Vocal Musick is also brought to the greatest Perfection of any Society perhaps in the Province:—Indeed, the Public seem not to be insensible of these Advantages; for, though it is said to be the largest Building erected for the publick Worship of God on the Continent, such Multitudes flock thither, of *all Denominations*, as very frequently not to find Room.

It would, I confess, be the highest Injustice in me here (and it would be paying the Audience but a poor Compliment) to insinuate, but that the Certainty of hearing a *spirited Discourse*, deliver'd with *a becoming Warmth and Energy*, and *enforced with that Dignity and Solemnity becoming the sacred Desk*, has its proper Weight with the Multitude who flock thither; but I do contend, that no House of Worship in *America* was ever so crouded before, except when the inimitable *Whitefield* graced the same.

The Members of the two *episcopal Churches* in this City, sensible of the Advantages cited in the preceding Pages, and encouraged by the Certainty of being able to get Organs made here in *as great Perfection* as in *England*, and near *one Half cheaper*, have lately rais'd suitable Contributions among themselves, with which to erect a very genteel one in their respective Churches; and many in the Country are following their laudable Example.

And would to God, that, divested of every Prejudice, this amiable Spirit of promoting the *decent Worship of* God would diffuse itself among the *Presbyterians* and *Baptists* also.—What a glorious Appearance would an Organ make in some of their Churches, especially in this and the neighbouring Cities! Nor would one look out of Character in the meanest Building in the Country.—We should not by this deviate more from the Faith of *true Presbyterianism*, than those of our Brethren in *Scotland*, *Ireland*, and *America* do, who have Steeples with Bells to their Churches (where they are of Ability) which are not only used at stated Times for Worship, Times of public Rejoicing, *&c.* but toll at the Death and Interment not only of their own Members, but Persons of any other Persuasion who request, and will go to the Expence of the same: The

Generality of our Clergy also in the *old Countries* wear the same decent Badges of Distinction (*viz.* the Gown and Band) with the Clergy of the Church of *England*; so that the introducing the Use of the *Organ* into our Acts of Worship, would not bring us one Jot nearer to *Popery* or *Episcopacy* than we were before, as some of our weak but well-meaning Professors may be apt to imagine.

Besides the Advantages cited in the preceding Pages, such an Institution would have this good Tendency, that, instead of their Members loitering away the blessed Sabbath Day at Home, sequestering themselves from the rest of Mankind in unsocial Retirements, or *crouding other Houses of Worship*, it would induce them to croud *their own*:—And, till this is taken *into Consideration*, they have, I fear, very little Grounds to expect their Congregations will either thrive or increase on their Hands.

Francis Hopkinson

Francis Hopkinson (1737-1791) was a signer of the Declaration of Independence, Judge of the Admiralty, poet, essayist, and amateur musician, whose song "My Days Have Been So Wondrous Free" (1759) is the earliest known secular music by an American composer. The letter that follows was written by Hopkinson to the Anglican rector of Philadelphia's Christ Church and St. Peter's "on the Conduct of a Church Organ," and gave practical advice on the place of the organ in the service and the kind of music that should be played on it.

Francis Hopkinson, "A Letter to the Rev. Doctor White, Rector of Christ Church and St. Peter's on the Conduct of a Church Organ" (1786). In Francis Hopkinson, *The Miscellaneous Essays and Occasional Writings* (Philadelphia: T. Dobson, 1792), vol. 2, 119-126.

I am one of those who take great delight in sacred music, and think, with royal David, that heart, voice, and instrument should unite in adoration of the great Supreme.

A soul truly touched with love and gratitude, or under the influence of penitential sorrow, will unavoidably break forth in expressions suited to its feelings. In order that these emanations of the mind may be conducted with uniformity and a becoming propriety, our church hath adopted into her liturgy, the book of psalms, commonly called *David's Psalms*, which contain a great variety of addresses to the Deity, adapted to almost every state and temperature of a devout heart, and expressed in terms always proper, and often sublime.

To give wings, as it were to this holy zeal, and heighten the harmony of the soul, *organs* have been introduced into the churches. The application of instrumental music to the purposes of piety is well known to be of very ancient date. Indeed, originally, it was thought that music ought not to be applied to any other purpose. Modern improvements, however, have discovered, that it may be made expressive of every passion of the mind, and become an incitement to levity as well as sanctity.

Unless the real design for which an organ is placed in a church be constantly kept in view, nothing is more likely to happen than an abuse of this noble instrument, so as to render it rather an obstruction to, than an assistant in, the good purpose for which the hearers have assembled.

Give me leave, sir, to suggest a few rules for the conduct of an organ in a place of worship, according to my ideas of propriety.

1st. The organist should always keep in mind, that neither the time or place is suitable for exhibiting all his powers of execution; and that the congregation have not assembled to be entertained with his performance. The excellence of an organist consists in his making the instrument subservient and conducive to the purposes of devotion. None but a master can do this. An ordinary performer may play surprising tricks, and shew great dexterity in running through difficult passages, which he hath subdued by dint of previous labour and practice. But *he* must have judgement and taste who can call forth the powers of the instrument, and apply them with propriety and effect to the seriousness of the occasion.

2nd. The voluntary, previous to reading the lessons, was probably designed to fill up a solemn pause in the service; during which, the clergyman takes a few minutes respite, in a duty too lengthy, perhaps, to be continued without fatigue, unless some intermission be allowed: there, the organ hath its part alone, and the organist an opportunity of shewing his power over the instrument. This, however, should be done with great discretion and dignity, avoiding every thing light and trivial; but rather endeavouring to compose the minds of the audience, and strengthen the tendency of the heart in those devout exercises, in which, it should be presumed, the congregation are now engaged. All sudden jirks, strong contrasts of *piano* and *forte*, rapid execution, and expressions of tumult, should be avoided. The voluntary should proceed with great chastity and decorum; the organist keeping in mind, that his hearers are now in the midst of divine service. The full organ should seldom be used on this occasion, nor should the voluntary last more than *five minutes* of time.

Some relaxation, however, of this rule may be allowed, on festivals and grand occasions.

3[d]. The *chants* form a pleasing and animating part of the service; but it should be considered, that they are not songs or tunes, but a species of *recitative*, which is no more than speaking musically. Therefore, as melody or song is out of the question, it is necessary that the harmony should be complete, otherwise *chanting*, with all the voices in unison, is too light and thin for the solemnity of the occasion. There should at least be half a dozen voices in the organ gallery to fill the harmony with bass and treble parts, and give a dignity to the performance. Melody may be frivolous; harmony, never.

4th. The prelude which the organ plays immediately after the psalm is given out, was intended to advertise the congregation of the psalm tune which is going to be sung; but some famous organist, in order to shew how much he could make of a little, has introduced the custom of running so many divisions upon the simple melody of a psalm tune, that the original purpose of this prelude is now totally defeated, and the tune so disguised by the fantastical flourishes of the dexterous performer, that not an individual in the congregation can possibly guess the tune intended, until the clerk has sung through the first line of the psalm. And it is constantly observable, that the full congregation never join in the psalm before the second or third line, for want of that information which the organ should have given. The tune should be distinctly given out by the instrument, with only a few chaste and expressive decorations, such as none but a master can give.

5th. The interludes between the verses of the psalm were designed to give the singers a little pause, not only to take breath, but also an opportunity for a short retrospect of the words they have sung, in which the organ ought to assist their reflections. For this purpose the organist should be previously informed by the clerk of the verses to be sung, that he may modulate his interludes according to the subject.

To place this in a strong point of view, no stronger, however, than what I have too frequently observed to happen; suppose the congregation to have sung the first verse of the 33[d] psalm.

"Let all the just to God with joy
Their chearful voices raise;
For well the righteous it becomes
To sing glad songs of praise."

How dissonant would it be for the organist to play a pathetic interlude in a flat third, with the slender and distant tones of the echo organ, or the deep and smothered sounds of a single diapason stop?

Or suppose again, that the words sung have been the 6th verse of the vi[th] psalm.

"Quite tired with pain, with groaning faint,
No hope of ease I see,
The night, that quiets common griefs
Is spent in tears by me"—

How monstrously absurd would it be to hear these words of distress succeeded by an interlude selected from the fag end of some thundering figure on a full organ, and spun out to a most unreasonable length? Or, what is still worse, by some trivial melody with a rhythm so strongly marked, as to set all the congregation to beating time with their feet or heads? Even those who may be impressed with the feelings such words should occasion, or in the least disposed for melancholy, must be shocked at so gross in impropriety.

The interludes should not be continued above 16 bars in *triple*, or ten or twelve bars in *common* time, and should always be adapted to the verse sung: and herein the organist hath a fine opportunity of shewing his sensibility, and displaying his taste and skill.

6th. The voluntary after service was never intended to eradicate every serious idea which the sermon may have inculcated. It should rather be expressive of that chearful satisfaction which a good heart feels under the sense of a duty performed. It should bear, if possible, some analogy with the discourse delivered from the pulpit; at least, it should not be totally dissonant from it. If the preacher has had for his subject, penitence for sin, the frailty and uncertainty of human life, or the evils incident to mortality, the voluntary may be somewhat more chearful than the tenor of such a sermon might in strictness suggest; but by no means so full and free as a discourse on praise, thanksgiving, and joy, would authorize.

In general, the organ should ever preserve its dignity, and upon no account issue light and pointed movements which may draw the attention of the congregation and induce them to carry home, not the serious sentiments which the service should impress, but some very petty air with which the organist hath been so good as to entertain them. It is as offensive to hear lilts and jiggs from a church organ, as it would be to see a venerable matron frisking through the public street with all the fantastic airs of a *columbine*.

Thomas Brattle

Thomas Brattle (1658-1713) was a successful Boston merchant and the brother of William Brattle, pastor of the Congregational church in Cambridge. Thomas was also the owner of one of the earliest organs in New England. The instrument, which was probably imported from England, and which he certainly owned by 1708, was kept in his home for his personal enjoyment. However, when Brattle died in 1713, his will (an extract from which is quoted below) bequeathed the organ to the Brattle Square Congregational Church, of which he was one of the founding members.

From Thomas Brattle, Will. Source: Henry Wilder Foote, *Annals of King's Chapel* (Boston: Little, Brown, 1882), vol. 1, 209.

I give, dedicate, and Devote my Organ to the praise and glory of God in the s^{d} Church [in Brattle Square], if they shall accept thereof, and within a year after my decease procure a Sober person that can play skilfully thereon with a loud noise. Otherwise to ye Church of England in this towne on ye same terms and conditions; and on their Non-acceptance or discontinuance as before I give the same to my Nephew William Brattle.

Brattle Square Church

The records of the Brattle Square Church indicate that the objections of New England Puritans to musical instruments were still quite strong, for the church refused to accept Brattle's gift. Indeed, it was not until 1790 that the Brattle Square congregation allowed an organ to be introduced into the church.

From church minutes, Brattle Square Congregational Society, July 24, 1713. Source: Foote, *Annals of King's Chapel*, vol. 1, 209.

July 24, 1713. The Rev. Mr. William Brattle, pastor of the church in Cambridge, signified by a letter the legacy of his brother, Thomas Brattle, Esq., late deceased, of a pair of organs, which he dedicated and devoted to the praise and glory of God with us, if we should accept thereof, and within a year after his decease procure a sober person skilful to play thereon. The church, with all possible respect to the memory of our deceased Friend and Benefactor, *Voted*, that they did not think it proper to use the same in the publick worship of God.

King's Chapel

As Brattle had obviously foreseen, the Brattle Square Church was likely to refuse his gift; thus, he had included a backup provision in his will to offer the organ to the Anglican congregation of King's Chapel, in which the Puritan objections to musical instruments were not operative. When the Brattle Square Church indeed turned down the organ, it was readily accepted by King's Chapel. Edward Enstone, whom the church attempted to secure as organist, was residing in England at the time. He accepted the church's offer and, by the end of 1714, was playing the Brattle organ in Boston's King's Chapel. To the further horror of the Puritans of Boston, Enstone also set himself up in the city as a teacher of dancing and music.

Extracts from church minutes, King's Chapel. Source: Foote, *Annals of King's Chapel*, vol. 1, 210-211.

At a meeting of the Gentlem of the Church this 3^{d} day of Augt 1713, Refering to the Orgains Giveing them by Thomas Brattle, Esqr: Dece^{d}, *Voted*, that the Orgins be Accepted by the Church, and that Mr Miles answer Mr William Brattle's Letter concerning the Same.

At a Vestry held at Boston Feb^{y}, 1713-14, *Voted*, that the Church Wardens write to Coll. Redknap and desire him to go to M^{r}. Edwd. Enston, who lives next Door to M^{r}. Master's on Tower Hill, and discourse him as to his Inclination and Ability to come over to be Organist here, We being willing to allow him Thirty p^{ds}: p Annum this money, which with other Advantages as to Dancing, Musick, etc., we doubt not will be sufficient Encouregement.

March 2^{d}, 1713-14, *Voted*, that the Organs be forthwith put up.

Ezra Stiles

Ezra Stiles (1727-1795) graduated from Yale in 1746 and was ordained in 1749. After studying law, he entered the ministry, becoming pastor of the Second Congregational Church in Newport, Rhode Island (1755). In 1778 he was appointed president and professor of ecclesiastical history at Yale. Stiles kept a detailed diary that sheds much light on various aspects of New England religious life during the late eighteenth century. On several occasions, Stiles noted the installation of an organ in an American church; his editorial comments on the subject reveal the typical Puritan disdain for instrumental music in worship.

Ezra Stiles, Diary. Source: *The Literary Diary of Ezra Stiles*, ed. Franklin Bowditch Dexter (New York: Charles Scribner's Sons, 1901), vol. 1, 57-58 (July 10, 1770).

10. Revd John Hubbard & Mr. Whitehead Hubb^{d} came. Last month an Organ of 200 Pipes was set up in the Meetinghouse of the first Congregational Chh. in Providence: and for the first time it was played upon in

divine Service last Ldsday [July 8, 1770], as Mr. Rowland the pastor tells me. This is the first organ in a dissenting presb. Chh. in America except Jersey College—or Great Britain.

Mr. Rowland tells me that since it was set up, a Providence Gentleman being at Elizabeth Town in the Jersies he was in comp[a] with Dr. Tho. Bradbury Chandler the episcopalian and mentioning that an organ was erected in Providence the Doctor said, he did not know but that they were entitled to a praemium—that a Gent. in Eng[ld] had by will left £500. ster. to the first dissenting Congreg[a] that should set up an organ. Also an English Gent. lately travell[g] thro. Providence told Mr. West the same Thing. I was at Provid. June 13 when the Organ was erected & setting up. Mr. Checkly who was concerned in psuading the p'ple. into it gave me an account of the motives he used with them, but said nothing of this Donation. They knew nothing about it when they erected the organ, & Mr. West had exercised himself upon it a month in learn[g] to play; before they knew, &c. However, they had the Information before July 8. Inst., when they first used it in public Worship. Mr. Rowland tells me it gives great offence to the Episcopalians in Prov. who say, we have nothing to do with it. Perhaps about ten years ago there was an Organ erected in Nassau Hall for the use of the Scholars at public prayers—on Ldsdays the college attend pub. Worship in the Meet[g] h. of the Town of Princetown. I then thought it an Innovation of ill consequence, & that the Trustees were too easily practised upon. They were a little sick of it. The organ has been disused for sundry years, & never was much used. In the year 1754 I saw in the *Dutch calvinist* Chh. at New York a small Organ, which was the first there & had been there I doubt not many years.

July 22, 1771 (ibid., vol. 1, 60).

22. Ldsdy. I preached at Providence in Mr. Rowland's Pulpit,[1] A.M.

[1] [Original editor's note] The following paragraph is from Dr. Stiles's Itinerary of this date:

The course of divine Service in the Congreg[a] Chh. at Providence under Rev. Mr. Rowland is this.—The Congregation rise & the Minister asks a Blessing on the Word & the divine presence in the Solemnities of public Worship—then the people sit, & the Minister reads a Chapter in the Bible—then the bills asking prayers &c are read by the Minister—then the Assembly rise & the Minister prays for a quarter & half an hour—then sing Watts Version of Psalms the people striking in with the Organ, & many sing standing, perhaps half the Congregation—then Minister takes a Text of Scripture, expounds it & preaches—the

2 Cor. vii, I. P.M. Jno vii, 37; the organ played on in Worship.

December 12, 1771 (ibid., vol. 1, 192).

12. An Organ is lately erected in the Episcopal called Kings Chh in Providence; and 10th Inst. at a church Assembly, notified by printed Hand Bills, it was first played on in divine Service, Rev. Jno Graves the Minister preaching a Sermon, & after that, a Contribution for the Expences. This I suppose was *Consecration* of the Organ. This Organ was taken from Concert-Hall in Boston—from being improved in promoting Festivity, Merriment, Effeminacy, Luxury & Midnight Revellings—to be used in the Worship of God. No Lecture at Mr. Hopk. this Evening.

May 16, 1785 (ibid., vol. 3, 162).

16. Visit^{g} my Flock. They have lately determined to set up an Organ in Dr Chauncys Meet^{g}house being the old Brick or first chh. in B^{o} founded 1629. The Doctor was against it, but Mr. Clark his Collegue & the Congreg^{a} in general were for it. This Spring the Meet^{g}house was repaired & D^{r} Ch. preached a Consecr^{a} & farewell Sermon on acc^{o} of his great age. The pple eager to get an Organ waited on the D^{r} who told them, that it would not be long before he was in his grave—he knew that before his head was cold there, they would have an Organ—and they might do as they pleased.

An Organ was erected in Nassau Hall, but there is none there now. A small house Organ was set up about 1768 in Mr. Rowlds Cong^{l} Meet^{g} in Providence, but it is now gone. These the only ones among the Presbyterians in America.

---

people sitting—Sermon being ended, the people rise & the Minister prays a short prayer—then singing & the Organ—then Minister pronounces the Blessing & dismisses the Congregation. But the Organ does not then play. This the Forenoon Service. The Afternoon the same, only in addition, between the last prayer & singing is the Contribution—& the last singing always concludes with the Xtian Doxology, & when it comes to the Doxology the whole Congregation rise & stand with great Solemnity. And after the Blessing is given, the Minister publishes the Banns of Marriage. The organ is a Chamber Organ, as large as a Desk & Book Case, containing about 200 Pipes. . . .

William Bentley

In addition to providing information about the use of the gallery orchestra in New England churches, the diary of William Bentley traces the increasing use of the organ among Congregationalists. Bentley's remarks indicate that he was not completely favorable to the use of the organ, but that it seemed to be necessary in view of the decline of vocal music in the congregations. The Brattle Street Church referred to under date of January 7, 1797, is the same as the Brattle Square Church that refused to accept Thomas Brattle's gift of an organ earlier in the century; now its "fine organ" was considered to be one of its most attractive features!

William Bentley, Diary. Source: *The Diary of William Bentley, D. D.* (Gloucester, Mass.: Peter Smith, 1962), vol. 1, 214 (November 20, 1790).

20. A Concert of music is proposed in St Peter's Church to be on the evening following thanksgiving. Tickets for the body of the Church at 1/6. The object is the repair of the Organ, which is now in the hands of a Dr Leavitt. The Band is to attend from Boston. Tickets are sent to the Clergy, for whom the Altar is reserved. After the advice of Dr Price & other dissenters, it is singular that on a day of devotion we should be so weak as to be betrayed into a justification of an act against the practice of dissenters, not only to hear organs in a Church, but to go on thanksgiving day to pay for the repairs of one for the service. This is beyond Catholic. If it is beneath the Pope to hear organs in the church, there might be some respect to heaven.

June 12, 1791 (ibid., vol. 1, 264).

I preached in Mr Clarke's congregation. It is not large, but very liberal in opinions. They have an organ, the first introduced into dissenting Meeting Houses. The example is seducing. Not merely from the fondness of parade, which leads religion, as well as follows easily in its train, but from the great inconveniences, & real difficulties attending the support of vocal Music. From my own experience I can say, that the greatest pains & expence cannot always ensure success.

August 7, 1791 (ibid., vol. 1, 283-284).

7. Sunday. Notes. Sarah Underwood for herself dangerously sick, & her two sons at Sea. We had no singing either in the morning or evening services. Two men singers came, & several women, but they would not

undertake. Mr Ward sung at the communion, & we have never failed in this part of our services. The expence has been great, & I regret that I shall be obliged to recant all I have against organs from mere necessity.

November 24, 1794 (ibid., vol. 2, 113).

24. Left Salem with Mr Priestley on a Journey to see the new Bridges of this County. . . . We reached Ipswich & were kindly received at Revd Dana's, for whom we carried Letters. . . . They have purchased an elegant organ for the first Church, of American manufacture.

January 7, 1797 (ibid., vol. 2, 211).

7. General Fiske had a shock of the Palsy, but he has so far recovered as to dine with his family this day. Madam D. tells us fine things of the growth of the Brattle Street Church. It continues to lead among the Congregational Churches. Its fine organ, charming voice of the Preacher, situation, & proprietors give it success. Madam Russel keeps up the generous attentions of her husband to the Minister & Society.

February 28, 1798 (ibid., vol. 2, 259).

28. Seriously engaged in the First Church upon the subject of an Organ. Subscriptions have already amounted to one thousand dollars. The absolute want of vocal musick is a plea which they can advance with justice. The first Organs were at Old Church in Boston, Dr. Clarke's, then at Brattle Street, Dr. Thacher's, then at the New South, Mr. Kirkland, tho' one was provided soon at the Bennet Street by the Universalists. A few years since one was purchased for the old Church in Newbury Port. I have heard of no other Congregational Churches. The old Church in Salem has has [sic] now made a subscription & an Organ will probably be obtained. There is a small one in the Cong. Church at Charlestown.

August 24, 1800 (ibid., vol. 2, 346).

24. Sunday. General Health. The old Church shut to prepare the Organ which is to be introduced for the first time into our worship in Salem.

January 22, 1801 (ibid., vol. 2, 362).

22. William Belstead, a famous musician, has died at Boston, aged 49. It is said that he has been Organist for Trinity Church in Boston 20 years. He was distinguished upon his violin which he often played when seemingly oppressed by sleep & utterly unable to answer to his name.

February 12, 1809 (ibid., vol. 3, 415-416).

12. Sunday. . . . The change of manners in our Order of the Church becomes every day more visible. An organ has been presented to the Congregational Church at Pittsfield under the pastoral care of the good republican Mr. Allen, by a Mr. Shearer. Organs are now used in our principal towns & in several towns in the County, perhaps as many as 12 in this state in Congregational Churches. 3 in Boston, 2 in Salem, 1 in Newbury Port.

David Benedict

David Benedict (1779-1874) was a New England Baptist pastor and historian, whose *A General History of the Baptist Denomination* (1813) provides not only historical accounts but also valuable information on the contemporary practices of this denomination. Another of Benedict's works, *Fifty Years among the Baptists* (1860), is more autobiographical in character. In the course of that book, Benedict found occasion to include a section on "The Introduction of the Organ among the Baptists," reproduced below.

From David Benedict, *Fifty Years among the Baptists* (New York: Sheldon & Company, 1860), 282-285.

The Introduction of the Organ among the Baptists.

This instrument, which from time immemorial has been associated with cathedral pomp and prelatical power, and has always been the peculiar favorite of great national churches, at length found its way into Baptist sanctuaries, and the first one ever employed by the denomination in this country, and probably in any other, might have been seen standing in the singing gallery of the old Baptist meeting house in Pawtucket, about forty years ago, where I then officiated as pastor; and in process of time, this *dernier resort* in church music was adopted by many of our societies which had formerly been distinguished for their primitive and conventicle plainness. The changes which have been experienced in the feelings of a large portion of our people has often surprised me. Staunch old Baptists in former times would as soon have tolerated the Pope of Rome in their pulpits as an organ in their galleries, and yet the instrument has gradually found its way among them, and their successors in church management, with nothing like the jars and difficulties which arose of old concerning the bass viol and smaller instruments of music.

The circumstances attending the innovation in question among my people, which was rather pleasing than offensive to the whole concern, may be thus related: As yet there was no other house of worship in the place, and our choir of singers were making vigorous efforts in behalf of their department, in connection with the Mozart Society, which for many years occupied an important position in the singing line, and frequently had concerts of a very popular character, which were always held in our house of worship. In aid of these performances a small organ was obtained by a joint-stock company, which, in the end, became a permanent fixture of the house. This clever little concern, still alive in another congregation, took the place of all the inferior cymbals on which our singers hitherto depended for instrumental aid, and by degrees became a favorite with all the people however much some of them had previously been biassed against any artificial aid in the melody of the sanctuary, and indeed, to the attractions of the gallery, rather than the pulpit, some people slyly ascribed the full houses which we generally enjoyed.

This change in Baptist policy happened in a suburban branch of the old Roger Williams church, at a distance of four miles from its center, a number of years before any movement was made by the mother body in the organ business.

I have already stated that at the time above referred to, the house in which I officiated was the only one in Pawtucket, or its vicinity, where are at present accommodations more or less splendid for church-going people of many different creeds. And I would furthermore state that for a number of years past, there have existed within my old parish bounds, six good houses of worship for Baptists, in all of which the instruments so indispensable for modern singers are found. One of this number is of the Freewill order, but this community a few years since, following in the wake of their brethren of a more stringent creed, placed an organ in their own singing gallery.

How far this modern organ fever will extend among our people, and whether it will on the whole work a *re*-formation or *de*-formation in their singing service, time will more fully develop. The original purpose of our small instrument was to assist the old-fashioned gallery choir, and to gather it in full strength around it, and so long as the musical concern in question is thus employed, we may reasonably expect it will be viewed with favor by spiritual worshipers, but whenever it shall assume an overwhelming influence, and only a few artistic performers be retained in the singers' seats, to be directed by men who take but little interest in any of the services of the sanctuary, except what pertains to their professional duty, then a machine, harmless in itself, will be looked upon with disfavor if not with disgust by the more pious portion of our assemblies.

12
The Churches of Christ Reject the Use of Instruments

THE early nineteenth century was a period of considerable religious ferment in the United States, a ferment that is often referred to as the Second Great Awakening. Local church revivals and a new venue, the campmeeting, led to rejuvenation of established churches like the Presbyterians, Methodists, and Baptists, and to the founding of new groups such as the Disciples of Christ. In contrast to the established denominations, which were in the process of introducing musical instruments into their services, the early Disciples rejected all forms of "mechanical music." In later years, many Disciples churches changed their stance on the instrument question, so that most churches of this communion now use them. However, the Church of Christ—which resulted from a split within the Disciples movement—has maintained a no-instruments policy to the present day.

Alexander Campbell

Alexander Campbell (1788-1866), together with his father, Thomas Campbell (1763-1854), was the chief leader in the founding of the Disciples of Christ during the early nineteenth century. Campbell and his followers stressed a return to New Testament Christianity, the union of all believers, the independence of local churches, and weekly communion, taking for their motto the words "Where the Scriptures speak, we speak; where the Scriptures are silent, we are silent." Since the New Testament is silent on the use of instruments for earthly worship, the early Disciples advocated their banishment from the service. The first part of the following item is quoted from an unnamed source; the last part is devoted to Campbell's tongue-in-cheek response.

Alexander Campbell, "Instrumental Music," *Millennial Harbinger*, ser. IV, vol. 1 (Bethany, Va.: A. Campbell, 1851), 581-582.

"Instrumental music is entirely in harmony with the most grateful, solemn and happy feelings of which the human heart is susceptible. Indeed, sacred music upon an instrument, tends, in a very considerable degree, to excite solemn and holy emotions; and we cannot forbear to say, that could the music of our churches be improved—could it be accompanied with an instrument, it would add very much to the solemnity of our worship; it would soothe and calm the feelings of the auditors; it would improve the order of the house; it would call into lively action the latent religious emotions of the heart, and add very much to the enjoyment on such occasions.

"Music exerts a mysterious charm upon man—it takes captive the citadel of life—carries him out of himself, and leads him where it will. The shrill fife and the rattling drum, inspire the soldier just about to enter into battle, with a zeal and daring which no hardship can overcome, and no danger intimidate, and causes him to rush headlong into the thickest of the combat, regardless of consequences. If martial music thus inspires the worshippers of Mars, will sacred music do less for the humble followers of the meek and lowly Jesus—the worshippers of the true and living God? No! It will not. It will inspire them, too, with zeal and courage, and impel them on to resist—not flesh and blood with instruments of death, but principalities and powers—spiritual wickedness in high places, with the armor of God and the sword of the Spirit. G."

The argument drawn from the Psalms in favor of instrumental music, is exceedingly apposite to the Roman Catholic, English Protestant, and Scotch Presbyterian churches, and even to the Methodist communities. Their churches having all the world in them—that is, all the fleshly progeny of all the communicants, and being founded on the Jewish pattern of things—baptism being given to all born into the world of these politico-ecclesiastic communities—I wonder not, then, that an organ, a fiddle, or a Jews-harp, should be requisite to stir up their carnal hearts, and work into ecstasy their animal souls, else "hosannahs languish on their tongues, and their devotions die." And that all persons who have no spiritual discernment, taste, or relish for their spiritual meditations, consolations and sympathies of renewed hearts, should call for such aid, is but natural. Pure water from the flinty rock has no attractions for the mere toper or wine-bibber. A little alcohol, or genuine Cogniac brandy, or good old Madeira, is essential to the beverage to make it truly refreshing. So to those who have no real devotion or spirituality in them, and whose animal nature flags under the oppression of church service, I think with Mr. G., that instrumental music would be not only a desideratum, but an essential prerequisite to fire up their souls to even animal devotion. But I presume, to all spiritually-minded Christians, such aids would be as a cow bell in a concert. A. C.

M. C. Kurfees

M. C. Kurfees (1856-1931) served as minister of Campbell Street Church of Christ, Louisville, Kentucky, and as associate editor and subsequently editor (1908-1924) of the *Gospel Advocate*. Kurfees wrote extensively on the "instrument question," particularly in a pamphlet, *Walking by Faith* (date of first edition not known), and a book, *Instrumental Music in the Worship: or the Greek Verb Psallo Philologically and Historically Examined* (1911), both of which have been reprinted many times. *Walking by Faith* originated as two sermons preached—probably several times—by Kurfees, one for the morning service and another for the same evening. In the passage from the morning sermon excerpted below, the author argues that musical instruments are forbidden in worship because they were not specifically enjoined in the New Testament, noting that there is nothing inherently harmful in the instruments themselves, but that only what God has directly commanded can be used in his service. In the second extract (from the evening sermon), he deals with the objection that, although musical instruments are not commanded by God in the New Testament, neither are "carpets, pews, baptisteries, chandeliers, and such like," all of which may be found in Churches of Christ.

From M. C. Kurfees, *Walking by Faith: Origin of Instrumental Music in Christian Worship*, 6th ed. (Nashville: Gospel Advocate, 1902), 8-14, 24-27.

First of all, the inspired Scriptures clearly set forth the fact that whenever and wherever persons attempted to do as service to God, either what He had forbidden or what He had not commanded, it was rejected. Through Samuel the prophet, the Lord issued a command to king Saul in the following words: "Now go and smite Amalek, and utterly destroy all that they have, and spare them not; but slay both man and woman, infant and suckling, ox and sheep, camel and ass." 1. Sam. xv. The record informs us that Saul smote the Amalekites from Havilah to Shur, but that he and the people took Agag the king alive, and spared the best of the sheep and oxen. That is, they followed their own wisdom in the matter. Further on, we will see why Saul did this, and that he has many successors and imitators to-day. When he and Samuel met, the disobedient king addressed Samuel thus: "Blessed be thou of the Lord; I have performed the commandment of the Lord." Samuel replied: "What meaneth, then, the bleating of the sheep and the lowing of the oxen which I hear?" Hoping to make amends for his wrong by offering a sacrifice, which had not been commanded, Saul replied: "The people spared the best of the sheep and oxen, to sacrifice unto the Lord thy God," adding further on, "I have obeyed the voice of the Lord, and have gone the way which the Lord sent me; . . . but the people took of the spoil to sacrifice unto the Lord thy God in Gilgal." The prophet of God replied: "Behold, to obey is better than sacrifice," showing that obedience consists in doing what is commanded, and that all service not commanded, though it be the sacrifice of the cattle upon a thousand hills, is vain worship. God's Word clearly reveals the fact that no kind of service which man may render to the Lord is acceptable, unless the Lord himself has ordered it. Gratuitous service is never acceptable to God. Seeing his great mistake, Saul now gives out the secret of his departure from the will of God in the following open confession: "I have sinned; I have transgressed the commandment of the Lord and thy word; because I feared the people and obeyed their voice." There it is. Saul yielded to the will of the people instead of maintaining loyalty to the will of God. The same spirit is abroad today. To keep abreast of denominational fashions, the people clamor for departures from the will of God, while lax and latitudinarian leaders in the pulpit yield to the popular demand. Instead of leading the people along the pathway of loyalty to the Lord, they are themselves led by the people to copy after the denominations around them. One divine purpose in placing elders over a church is to guard against false teaching (Acts xx. 28-31; Tit. i. 7-11), but unfortunately in many instances, instead of maintaining a loyal stand by the Word of God, thus showing the young and uninstructed that it is wrong to follow the wisdom of men, the elders themselves yield to the imperious demand of the young people.

The schismatic and subversive scheme of Korah, Dathan, and Abiram, Num. xvi, is another illustration in point. God's order was that Aaron and his sons should burn incense, while the Levites, to whom Korah and his company belonged, had other duties assigned them. Becoming tired of God's order, they protested to Moses that he and Aaron were assuming too much authority, and that they had as much right to burn incense as Aaron and his sons. To carry out their scheme more effectively, they gathered together "two hundred and fifty princes of the assembly, famous in the congregation, men of renown." Here were two hundred and fifty of the most prominent men among the people taking counsel against the Lord's order. Conventions and councils have been the hot-beds of heresy in all ages. The present instance was not an exception to the rule. Seeing they were determined to carry out their purposes, Moses told them to get ready with their censers, and then added: "Hereby ye shall know that the Lord hath sent me to do all these works; for I have not done them of mine own mind: if these men die the common death of all men, . . . then the Lord hath not sent me; but if . . . the earth open her mouth and swallow them up, . . . then ye shall understand that these men have provoked the Lord." No sooner had Moses delivered this loyal speech, than the earth clave asunder and swallowed up Korah and all his company. The Lord had just spoken words of warning to Moses and Aaron, and through them to the congregation, saying, "Separate yourselves from among this congregation; . . . depart, I pray you, from the tents of these wicked men, . . . lest ye be consumed in all their sins," thus teaching the solemn lesson that, when men deliberately depart from the will of God, we should separate ourselves from them. Through Paul, in Rom. xvi. 17, the New Testament enjoins the same duty: "I beseech you, brethren, mark them who are causing divisions and occasions of stumbling, contrary to the doctrine which ye learned, and turn away from them." This is the commandment of an inspired apostle of Christ.

Thus, we see there are but two ways, in general terms, to treat God's order—either obey it, or disobey it. Obedience consists in doing what God says, no more and no less. Disobedience consists in any departure from God's order, whether it be doing what He forbids, omitting all or a part that He commands, doing as religious service what He does not command, or in any modification of His will.

Let us now view this principle in the light of New Testament facts. According to the teaching of Jesus, the same principle holds good in the service of God to-day. It is still true that *whenever and wherever men do, as religious service, what they are not commanded to do, it is rejected.* But there is a broad distinction between doing a thing *as religious service*, and doing the same thing outside of religious service. As already observed at another point, an act wholly harmless in itself when done outside of religious service, may be very harmful when done in religious service. In the light of some specifications, the correctness of this principle will clearly appear.

1. *Washing the hands.* In this, there is nothing wrong in the mere act

itself, as all can see, and yet it is one of the very acts which Jesus condemned in the strongest terms (Mark vii. 3, 7). But why did He condemn it? Look at the question from every possible point of view, and the only correct answer is, it was condemned because they were doing, as religious service, something which, although right itself, had not been commanded.

2. *Eating meat.* Is it wrong to eat meat? You answer, no. Then, suppose we place it on the Lord's table with the bread and wine? You are ready to say, that would not be right. Why not? You can neither say, it is because the act is wrong in itself, nor because it is forbidden; for we not only know it is not wrong to eat meat, but that God has no where said we must not eat it on His table. As in the former case, so here, there is only one correct answer, and that is, the wrong consists in the fact *that the Lord has not told us to do so.*

3. *Infant baptism.* Is it wrong to baptize infants? If so, why? Certainly not because it is wrong to apply water to infants, nor to dip them in water. It is true, God has commanded believer's baptism, but, notwithstanding this fact, it would still be right to practice both, as has been done, if God had cammanded [sic] it. The practice is wrong, therefore, not because the act itself is sinful apart from religious service, but because there is no divine authority for the act in religious service.

4. *Instrumental music.* Is it wrong to play on musical instruments? Here again we must reply, there is nothing wrong in the act itself outside of religious service. The opposition to instrumental music in the worship is misunderstood by many good people. They often say: "Instrumental music is so attractive and entertaining in its effect that we can not see why anyone should oppose it." If this were the criterion of judgment, the opposition would cease at once. Its use in the worship of God is not opposed on the ground that there is no taste for the music itself. The bewitching strains of the organ, piano, violin, etc., are equally as pleasing and attractive to many of the opponents as they are to any who advocate its use. Why, then, oppose it? Simply because God has not appointed it in His worship, but has appointed music of another kind. God has no more plainly said, eat bread on the Lord's table than He has said use vocal music in the worship. In Eph. v. 19, Paul says: "Speaking to yourselves in psalms and hyms [sic] and spiritual songs, singing and making melody in your heart to the Lord"; and in Col. iii. 16: "Let the word of Christ dwell in you richly in all wisdom; teaching and admonishing one another with psalms and hymns and spiritual songs, singing with

grace in your hearts unto God"; and Jesus and His disciples sang a hymn at the institution of the Lord's Supper, Matt. xxvi. 30. Hence, by both precept and example, vocal music is appointed in the worship of God. It is sometimes argued from Rev. v. 8, and xiv. 2, that there will be instrumental music in heaven; but what of it? There will be infant membership there, too; and the same passage speaks of "golden bowls of incense." If the Lord provides for infant membership and instrumental music in heaven, it will be right for them to be there; but if He excludes both from the church on earth, we should do the same. God's will should be man's guide.

But it is claimed that the Lord has not forbidden instrumental music. Neither has He forbidden meat on the Lord's table, except by telling us to eat something else; and in the same way He has forbidden instrumental music by telling us to use another kind. If specifying what we are to eat on the Lord's table excludes everything else, then specifying what kind of music we are to use in worship, excludes every other kind. If not, why not? Here, then, are four distinct acts—*washing the hands*, *eating meat*, *dipping an infant in water*, and *playing on musical instruments*, all of which are sinless in themselves, but wrong when done as religious acts, because there is no divine authority for it. The worship of God was not appointed as an æsthetical performance to please and gratify man's taste, but to please and honor God by loyalty to His Word. We are to walk by faith. . . .

The following objections are sometimes urged:

1. That there is no specific command for carpets, pews, pulpits, baptisteries, chandeliers, and such like, and if it is not wrong to have these things, neither is it wrong to have instrumental music. But, the fact that these things are not named in the Bible is certainly no proof that something else not named therein is allowable; and, since some things not specifically named are, nevertheless, necessarily implied, it does not follow that because one thing not so named is allowable, therefore, another is. Be it distinctly understood, however, that if these things, like instrumental music, were a part of the worship, as we shall see further on that the latter is, it would be equally wrong to have them. It is wrong to do any thing as worship to God which he does not command. But the cases are by no means parallel. The act performed in a baptistery is an act which God commands; but the act performed in playing on a musical instrument is an act which God does not command. Moreover, the act of baptism performed in a baptistery is the same act whether performed in

a baptistery, a river, a lake, or a pond; but the act performed on a musical instrument is not the same act which is performed in singing, and which God commands. Singing and playing are two distinct acts; each can exist without the other, and God commands the one, but not the other. Those who play on musical instruments in Christian worship are, therefore, doing what God has no where commanded them to do. But, whether we baptize in a baptistery, preach the Word in a pulpit, listen to it while sitting in a pew with or without as "many lights" burning as when Paul preached in Troas (Acts xx. 8), or sing God's praises while the feet rest on a carpeted or carpetless floor, we are in each case performing the act which God commands; but, in playing on a musical instrument we are not performing an act which God commands. In other words, we can not baptize in a baptistery, preach the Word in a pulpit, listen to it in a pew, or sing God's praises in a house with or without a carpet or lights, without doing in each case what God commands; but we can play on a musical instrument without doing any thing which God commands. If it be said we can not sing psalms accompanied by a musical instrument without doing what God commands, I reply, this would not only be doing what God commands, but more than He commands; and if it be further claimed that in singing psalms accompanied by an instrument we are no more doing more than is commanded than when we preach in a pulpit, I reply that the cases are not parallel for the reason that the pulpit or its equivalent—a place to occupy while preaching—is necessarily implied in the command to preach, since this command can not be obeyed without being obeyed *in some place*; but neither a musical instrument nor its equivalent is implied in the command to sing, since this command can be obeyed without playing on an instrument or doing anything equivalent to it. Place is a necessary incidental in obeying the commands to preach, hear preaching, baptize, and sing; but instrumental music is not a necessary incidental in obeying the command to sing. It is another kind of music which may or may not accompany vocal music. In preaching, we are not compelled to have a pulpit, we are compelled to have its equivalent—a place to occupy; in hearing preaching we are not compelled to have pews, but we are compelled to have their equivalent—a place to occupy; we are not compelled to have a carpeted floor, but we are compelled to have some kind of a floor wherever we worship, and no kind is specified either with or without a carpet; we are not compelled to have a baptistery, but we are compelled to have its equivalent—a place in which to baptize. Such things are not explicitly, but implicitly commanded. The only reason, therefore, that these things or their equivalents are contended for is because they are necessarily implied in what is commanded, and we are compelled to have them; but instrumental music is not implied in the command to sing, and we are neither compelled to have it nor anything equivalent to it. The attempt to classify these things together is, therefore, a pitiable subterfuge.

13
The Organ in Nineteenth-Century Scotland

JOHN Knox, the sixteenth-century founder of the Scottish Presbyterian church, had been greatly influenced by John Calvin. In musical matters, this meant that Scottish Presbyterian worship was restricted to unison a cappella singing of metrical psalms. These strictures began to break down in English and American Presbyterian churches during the late eighteenth and early nineteenth centuries, but it was to be nearly another hundred years before the organ began to make inroads into the Scottish churches. Significantly, it was not the example of any of the great liturgical churches that made the organ acceptable to Scottish Presbyterians, but the influence of an American musical evangelist.

Ira D. Sankey

Ira D. Sankey (1840-1908) was the musical half of the famous Moody-Sankey revival team of the late nineteenth century. In 1873 Sankey and Dwight L. Moody began an evangelistic tour of the British Isles, where Sankey made considerable use of gospel songs sung as solos, accompanying himself at a portable organ. This caused the singer some concern when the team was in Scotland, for many of the Scottish churches still objected to the use of musical instruments, as well as hymns of "human composure." On the whole, however, Sankey and his instrument seem to have been readily accepted and probably went a good way toward breaking down the resistance to the use of organs among the Scotch.

From Ira D. Sankey, *My Life and the Story of the Gospel Hymns* (New York and London: Harper & Brothers, 1907), 44-46, 57-63.

Among other invitations was one from a minister at Sunderland, the Rev. A. A. Rees. Mr. Moody, fearing that in this case there might also be some trouble in regard to "penny collections," sent me to the place to learn the situation. Mr. Rees met me at the station, and I remained with him over night. During the evening he made a number of inquiries about Mr. Moody, and said that a year or so ago he had met a man in Ireland with the name of Moody, and that if this was the same man, he desired very much to have him come and preach in his chapel. His reason for this was, that in the home of a Mr. Bewley, he had been assigned to share a bedroom with Mr. Moody, and before retiring Moody suggested that they have evening devotions, and that he had never heard anything that equaled Mr. Moody's prayer and burning desire for a greater knowledge of God's Word and power to preach it. On assuring him that this was the same man, it was at once settled that we should come the next week, and that there should be no "penny collections" to interfere with the work.

Almost immediately after arriving Mr. Rees requested me to go with him to the home of Mr. Longstaff, treasurer of Mr. Rees' chapel, and the man who many years afterward wrote the hymn, "Take time to be holy." On entering the parlor I discovered an American organ in a corner of the room, which, I was told, had been used by Philip Phillips in his service of song in that city. I was requested to sing, which I did, not knowing that the minister was strongly opposed, not only to solo singing, but to organs and choirs as well, never allowing anything of the kind in his church. Among the songs that I sang on this occasion I recall the following: "Come home, O Prodigal," "Free from the law," and "More to follow." The minister made no comments, but seemed much interested in the singing. A few days after our arrival in the city we were surprised to see the walls and billboards placarded with enormous posters, containing the following notice: "D. L. Moody of Chicago will preach the gospel, and Ira D. Sankey of Chicago will sing the gospel in Bethesda Chapel every afternoon and evening this week, except Saturday, at 3 and 7 o'clock. All are welcome." Thus the phrase, "sing the gospel" originated with one of the most conservative ministers in England.

We soon learned that we were in the hands of a pastor who was known throughout that section as "the pope of the north," and that none of the other ministers had been asked to join in the services. For the first time in the history of that chapel a small cabinet organ was not only brought in, but given conspicuous place in the large pulpit, from which place I was better able to command the galleries and lead the singing than would have been the case had the organ occupied a place on the floor below. . . .

Our first meeting in Edinburgh was advertised to be held on Sunday evening, November 23, and long before the hour for commencing the service arrived the whole building was densely packed to its utmost corners; even the lobbies, stairs and entrance were crowded with people, while more than two thousand were turned away.

The first announcement made was a sad disappointment to the congregation, for it was that Mr. Moody could not be present, he having contracted a severe cold the day before, while on the train en route from Carlisle. It was further announced that Mr. Sankey would conduct the service of song, and the Rev. J. H. Wilson would preach.

This was indeed a trying hour for the singer. Much had been said and written in Scotland against the use of "human hymns" in public worship, and even more had been uttered against the employment of the "kist o' whistles," the term by which they designated the small cabinet organ I employed as an accompaniment to my voice.

A goodly number of ministers and prominent laymen were present. After the opening prayer I asked all to join in singing a portion of the One Hundredth Psalm. To this they responded with a will, as it was safe and common ground for all denominations, and no questions were raised as to Mr. Rouse having introduced anything "human" into David's version as found in the Bible. This was followed by reading the Scriptures and prayer.

The service having been thus opened in regular order, we now faced the problem of "singing the gospel"—a term first devised and used by the Rev. Arthur A. Rees, of Sunderland, England, some months before in advertising our meetings in that city, and since then much discussed in Scotland. The song selected for my first solo was "Jesus of Nazareth passeth by."

The intense silence that pervaded that great audience during the singing of this song at once assured me that even "human hymns," sung in a prayerful spirit, were indeed likely to be used of God to arrest attention and convey gospel truth to the hearts of men in bonny Scotland, even as they had in other places.

After a powerful address by Dr. Wilson, and a closing prayer, I was requested to sing another solo. Selecting "Hold the Fort," then comparatively new in Edinburgh, the audience was requested to join in singing the chorus, "Hold the fort, for I am coming," which they did with such heartiness and such power that I was further convinced that gospel songs would prove as useful and acceptable to the masses in Edinburgh as they had in the cities of York and Newcastle in England.

In our meetings held prior to entering Scotland, it had been our custom to have the committee in charge of the various meetings—often three and four, in different localities, in a day—see that organs were placed in the halls and chapels ready for use. In Edinburgh we failed to inform the committee that upon them would devolve the matter of placing the organs in each hall and church as needed. The consequence of this oversight was that at our second meeting, held in Barclay Free Church, there was no organ provided, and therefore we could have no solo singing or gospel hymns.

When the committee discovered, about the hour for commencing the service, that the organ was not present, but away off at the Music Hall, they sent after the missing instrument, which was brought with great speed.

They hoped to arrive at the meeting in season for the closing exercises, and this end they certainly would have attained had not the Jehu in charge been over zealous in the use of his whip. In whirling round a corner near the church at too great a speed he overturned the vehicle, rolling both deputation and "kist o' whistles" into the middle of the street.

The "kist" was in a sadly demoralized condition, and its appearance now strangely suggestive of its Scotch name. The outcome of the disaster was that Mr. Moody had to conduct the second meeting alone, as I had led the first alone.

These occurrences evidently greatly pleased some of the Scotch folks, as they were heard to say: "It had a fine tendency to break up any scheme the evangelists might have had in their working together."

The third meeting was held in the same church, and great interest was manifested by the citizens. The question of the solo singing, as to its propriety and usefulness, was not as yet fully understood or admitted; hence it was with much fear and trepidation that we thus really entered, this third night, upon our three months' campaign.

As I took my seat at the instrument on that, to me, most memorable evening, I discovered, to my great surprise, that Dr. Horatius Bonar was seated close by my organ, right in front of the pulpit. The first gospel-song music I had ever composed, written since coming to Edinburgh, was set to words which he wrote—"Yet there is room."

Of all men in Scotland he was the one man concerning whose decision I was most solicitous. He was, indeed, my ideal hymn-writer, the prince among hymnists of his day and generation. And yet he would not sing one of his own beautiful hymns in his own congregation, such as, "I heard the voice of Jesus say," or, "I was a wandering sheep," because he ministered to a church that believed in the use of the Psalms only.

With fear and trembling I announced as a solo the song, "Free from the Law, oh, happy condition."

No prayer having been offered for this part of the service, and feeling that the singing might prove only an entertainment, and not a spiritual blessing, I requested the whole congregation to join me in a word of prayer, asking God to bless the truth about to be sung.

In the prayer my anxiety was relieved. Believing and rejoicing in the glorious truth contained in the song, I sang it through to the end.

At the close of Mr. Moody's address, Dr. Bonar turned toward me with a smile on his venerable face, and reaching out his hand he said: "Well, Mr. Sankey, you sang the gospel to-night."

And thus the way was opened for the mission of sacred song in Scotland.

At one of the meetings here a young man anxious to gain admittance to the already over-crowded hall, cried out to Mr. Moody: "I have come twenty miles to hear you, can't you make room for me somewhere?" Moody calmly replied: "Well, if we push the walls out you know what the roof will do."

On another occasion, as we were holding meetings in the Free Assembly Hall, while I was singing a solo a woman's shrill voice was heard in the gallery, as she made her way toward the door, crying: "Let me oot! Let me oot! What would John Knox think of the like of you?" At the conclusion of the solo I went across the street to sing at an overflow meeting in the famous Tolbooth Church. I had just begun to sing, when the same voice was again heard, "Let me oot! Let me oot! What would John Knox think of the like of you?"

Professor Blaikie said in the Edinburgh Daily Review at this time: "It is almost amusing to observe how entirely the latent distrust of Mr. Sankey's "kist o' whistles" has disappeared. There are different ways of using the organ. There are organs in some churches for mere display, as some one has said, 'with a devil in every pipe;' but a small harmonium, designed to keep the tune right, is a different matter, and is seen to be no hindrance to the devout and spiritual worship of God."

John Spencer Curwen

The influence of Sankey and other factors led to a growing acceptance of organs in Scottish churches of the late nineteenth century, a fact that is reflected in the writing below. John Spencer Curwen (1847-1916) was the son of John Curwen, the popularizer of the tonic sol-fa method of sight singing in England. Continuing his father's work, John Spencer also became one of the most important British music publishers of his time. He wrote two significant books on church music, *Studies in Worship Music* (1880) and *Studies in Worship Music, Second Series* (1885), which contain much valuable information on contemporary developments in sacred music in Great Britain. The following extract, originally delivered as part of a lecture in Glasgow, Scotland, in February 1883, provides pro and con arguments relative to the use of the organ in the Presbyterian churches of Great Britain.

From John Spencer Curwen, "Presbyterian Church Music." In *Studies in Worship Music (Second Series)* (London: J. Curwen & Sons, [1885], 78-79, 85-87.

It is a strong proof of the vitality of religious feeling in the Presbyterian Church that so keen a contest rages over the forms and methods of worship. If the champions of use and wont were content with a feeble and passive protest against innovations; if the younger and reforming spirits were satisfied to hint at reforms which they had not zeal enough to carry through, then we might indeed say that religion was in a bad way. Life, though it brings conflict sometimes is better than deadness, and universal agreement in details is a thing not at all to be desired.

What is, however, most earnestly to be desired is that we should approach this question of worship-music in a large and devout spirit, scorning littleness and repartee, striving to rise to high ground, and to discover the ultimate principles on which the application of music to worship rests.

It has been said, for example, that Presbyterians ought to make their services more artistic and musical, because the young people in the towns are going off to the Episcopal churches, where they can get these things. This seems to me a very poor argument. If, as I believe, it is right that we should freely admit art in so far as it serves the ends of worship, then let us advocate its introduction upon the distinct basis of principle, and not because we fear a stampede.

Again, I have read that organs ought to be allowed in churches because David played the harp; and I have seen special stress laid upon the fact that one of the earliest Scottish psalters has on its title-page a picture of the Psalmist outraging Presbyterian tradition by giving the Psalms with instrumental accompaniment. All this seems to me mere trifling. If organs are lawful and expedient, it is not because their counterparts were used in the Temple, but because they help to kindle heart and voice in God's praise. If they are unlawful and inexpedient, it is not because Presbyterian tradition is against them, but because they are not found to aid our worship. . . .

The church music question of greatest magnitude at the present day relates to the organ. At the very mention of the word the mildest person in this room becomes a partisan, so that a dispassionate study of the *pros* and *cons* of the matter is exceedingly difficult. The opponents of organs have entrenched themselves in a citadel, and they seem to be of opinion that if their citadel falls, the whole order of Presbyterian worship falls too. Meanwhile, the besiegers—armed, I suppose, with organ pipes instead of trumpets—are doing their best to bring down the walls. The capitulation is only a question of time.

Yet though we may smile at the heat and exaggeration which this controversy excites, there can be no doubt that the change from unaccompanied to accompanied singing is a serious and considerable one, involving great possibilities of harm to what we all so earnestly desire—congregational singing. Let us discuss the matter on practical grounds, setting aside arguments about lawfulness which even religious men feel to be out of harmony with the spirit of the times.

What is the effect of an organ upon congregational singing? I think it makes the act of singing easier, especially if you are trying to sing a part. The notes you want are in the atmosphere. Even though the instrument be so softly played as not to be heard, it is *felt* in the support it gives to the voices. I do not think it can be said to prevent flattening. Most of us have had painful experience that a congregation will flatten in spite of an organ, and will go on verse after verse, at its own flat pitch against the instrument in a way that tortures the ear. Flattening is not so frequent with an organ as without, but the organ does not cure the evil.

It is this function of affording a back-ground for the voices that an organ should perform. It should never attempt to lead. Many people seem to be of opinion that if an organ is introduced to a church the singing will at once improve, and need never trouble them again. What folly! As well might they expect to increase the piety of a congregation by building a tall steeple. Just as much pains must be taken with the vocal praise with an organ as without. There must be choir-practices and elementary singing-classes and never-ceasing work if a full and harmonious offering of praise is to be maintained.

So far we have spoken of organs as they *should* be used. But how are they commonly used in England, where they are universal and long established? They are often played so loudly that the choir and congregation chirp like birds in a thunderstorm. Moreover the organ is a very noble instrument, which engrosses all the energies and sympathies of the player. The organist, in ninety-nine cases out of a hundred, is the choirmaster, and does whatever other musical work is done in the congregation. He is absorbed in his instrument, and, in consequence, choir-training is neglected, and congregational training never thought of. Singing becomes shouting, the words are drowned in a muddy sea of organ tone, and the general result is noise, not music.

The organ is a good servant, but a bad master, and the temper of many of the intelligent opponents of organs is this—Let us bear the ills we have rather than fly to others that we know not of. I can assure you that the example of what has happened in England is enough to make me feel much sympathy with this position.

One word to the opponents of organs. A mere negative attitude is not enough. You must have a positive policy, and show people that you can produce an unaccompanied service which satisfies the ear and the devotional feeling richly and deeply, falling like the echoes of a purer worship upon the weary and distracted spirit.

The work necessary to create and sustain a service of this kind is far greater than for one which is accompanied. But it is work in aid of devotion, and if your opposition to organs springs really from your zeal for purity of worship, here is your opportunity of proving it.

Part V
The Twentieth Century

14
The Piano in American Musical Evangelism

IN the same way that the organ was introduced into Scottish Presbyterian churches, through its use in the evangelistic meetings of Moody and Sankey, the piano came to play an important role in many American congregations through the influence of later revival musicians, particularly Charles M. Alexander. Other factors certainly eased the way for the piano, including its inexpensiveness, ready availability, and simple playing technique—at least in comparison with the pipe organ. However, the example set by Alexander and his accompanists certainly commended the piano to the more evangelistic communions and led to the development of a "gospel style" of playing.

Helen C. Alexander and J. Kennedy Maclean

Charles M. ("Charlie") Alexander (1867-1920) was one of Ira D. Sankey's successors in the field of evangelistic music. Associated primarily with evangelists R. A. Torrey and especially J. Wilbur Chapman, Alexander led the music for meetings in Australia, the United States, and England during the early years of the twentieth century. The opposite of the somewhat reserved Sankey, Alexander served as a sort of master of ceremonies, leading congregations and choirs with flamboyant conducting gestures, interspersed with jokes, stories, and testimonies. Though not a composer himself, Alexander obtained the copyrights for many popular gospel songs of the time, including "His Eye is on the Sparrow," "One Day," and "Ivory Palaces." One of Alexander's innovations that was to have a significant impact on gospel hymnody and the worship of churches that used this style was his preference for the piano rather than the organ in his crusades. The pianist who accompanied Alexander for many of these crusades was the Australian Robert Harkness, who developed a style of evangelistic piano playing that is still in use today.

From Helen C. Alexander and J. Kennedy Maclean, *Charles M. Alexander: A Romance of Song and Soul-Winning* (London: Marshall Brothers, [1920]), 53, 55, 78-79, 199-200.

The choir for these services in the Exhibition Building [Melbourne, Australia, 1902] was composed of twelve hundred and fifty singers. Alexander did not care to use the great organ, which he preferred as a solo instrument, but substituted two pianos, finding that the quick, incisive notes of a piano held the singing of a large crowd together far better, and did not detract from the value of vocal harmonies like an organ. . . .

From June 14th to 18th [1902], Dr. Torrey and his associate were in Bendigo [Australia], and here, for the first time, Alexander met the young musician, Robert Harkness, who was to become his pianist for the next twelve years, and whose songs were to reach all over the world. Mr. Harkness had been appointed accompanist for the mission. His father, of good old English stock, had been Mayor of Bendigo more than once, and was famous in the locality as a man who had not feared to stand squarely on his Christian principles while in office. Alexander was drawn to the young musician from the first. They had no opportunity for private conversation on spiritual matters until the last day of the mission. Then they had a serious talk, which Mr. Harkness somewhat resented, refusing to come to an immediate decision. But Alexander's kindly manner, as they descended the stairs together, touched him. They parted at the door, and Mr. Harkness took his bicycle to start for home. Suddenly Alexander called out from the cab he was entering, "Come down to the train at three o'clock this afternoon, and go up to Maryborough with me for a week." Mr. Harkness agreed, and on his way home decided to accept the Saviour. When he joined Alexander at the railway station he was a new man in Christ Jesus.

From that day onwards, he became Alexander's second self in the music. He learned to know every piece in the red song-book, and as soon as a number was given out, he would strike the first chord on the piano. So closely did leader and pianist work together, that they often seemed fused into one, without any need of spoken directions. This fusion was not reached immediately, but was the result of constant work together, day after day, through the years. . . .

The weather [in Birmingham, England, 1904], which seemed at its worst, had little or no effect on the attendance of the throngs which grew denser as the weeks passed, and although both Dr. Torrey and Charles

Alexander caught heavy colds, which would have laid most men low, the work was not checked.

Special prayer meetings were held, and God marvellously gave to their voices power to carry on, in spite of all. Just as Alexander began to find the strain of the solo work well-nigh impossible, unexpected help was supplied by the arrival of Mr. J. Raymond Hemminger, who had been sent over from America to study the directing of Gospel music, and solo work, under Alexander. The song "God is now willing, are you?" will always be remembered in Birmingham as his most telling appeal. The marvellous playing of Robert Harkness, as he accompanied the immense volume of congregational singing under the magical skill of the songleader, aroused much interest among many lovers of music in Birmingham. Often-times it seemed as though the solitary grand piano was turned into a whole orchestra, as every part of its keyboard seemed to speak at once, from the deep rhythmic bass, which boomed like drums, to the flute-like tones of the upper notes, which floated in counter melodies above the swelling waves of eight thousand or more voices. Such old familiar hymns as "Shall we gather at the river?" seemed re-born, while the newer ones, such as "Never lose sight of Jesus," "It's just like Him," or "Loyalty to Christ," were echoed in streets, factories, and homes. . . .

During the Christmas holidays [of 1913] some changes took place in the personnel of the mission party. Albert Brown, of Nottingham, a fine Christian man, with a magnificent, well-trained baritone voice, was definitely appointed as Alexander's soloist in the place of E. W. Naftzger, whose health had temporarily broken down. Robert Harkness, who had been Alexander's right hand as pianist for twelve years, felt that he must settle into a home of his own, and took up business in London. The parting was a severe wrench after so long a time of intimate association in the Lord's work. Alexander tried for a time to obtain another pianist through the ordinary means of advertising. Several men of high ability and with wide experience as church organists endeavoured to fill the position, but the standard of the work needed was too severe a test. It required a peculiar adaptability of temperament, a quickness of resource, an exercise of memory powers, and of fine intuition, rarely possessed by even experienced musicians who have been trained along mechanical lines.

The curiously rigid, cut-and-dried attitude of many of the British people towards the music of hymns and sacred songs often causes a misunderstanding in the use of "Gospel Song" music, the rhythm of which is distinctively American. Because it is unfamiliar, it is sometimes treated with scant courtesy. The phrasing, which is the soul of "Gospel music," and which would be accorded to any other kind of musical composition, is often entirely disregarded, the piece rattled off without thought, and contemptuously thrown aside as a "mere jig." Unfortunately, some who love Gospel songs, and the message they contain, murder the music of them just as much, through ignorance of right phrasing, and by playing them all at a uniform high rate of speed. Another cause of misunderstanding arises in the use of syncopation, which, when properly employed, is not only effective in musical expression, but often helps to bring out the force of the words, which, after all, is the main purpose of religious music. The "coon-songs" which often pass in England for the music of the coloured people of the South, and the modern use of "rag-time" often cause a similar rhythm to be applied to Gospel songs, and this introduces a cheapness and levity that destroys all beauty in the song. But it takes time to learn and understand the right way of using this form of sacred music, and Alexander realized that the kind of double-harness work which twelve years had developed between himself and Harkness could not be immediately accomplished by one strange to his particular methods. But although never impatient, he was quick to see whether the ability was latent or not, and, after testing several applicants, he came to the conclusion that the usual avenues of advertisement were not of much value in finding him the right pianist.

Going one day into the London Headquarters of the Y.M.C.A. to call on his old friend J. J. Virgo, Alexander asked whether any of the young men were specially fond of piano-playing. "We are rather short of good musicians just now," replied Virgo, "but there is one fellow who is always playing around on the piano—'Barrie,' the others call him. I believe he is here now. Shall we go and see?" Mr. Virgo opened the door of his office, and the two entered the Lounge. A gust of laughter, and the sound of men's voices in song, greeted them. Seated at the piano was a short, stocky young man, with dark hair and spectacles, playing a rollicking song for the group of young fellows crowded closely around him. They were all enjoying themselves immensely, and at the sound of Mr. Virgo's voice the pianist turned with a broad and beaming smile. "I want you to meet Mr. Alexander," said Virgo. After a general handshake all round, Alexander asked the young men to go on singing, and finally arranged an interview with Mr. Barraclough. Finding that he was on the point of resigning from his position as secretary to a member of Parliament, Alexander invited him to come to Scotland for a week or two as his guest, to help him with stenography, piano accompaniments, or anything that was needed. Mr. Barraclough gladly consented, and spoke of the desire he had always had to make more use of his music, and to give his time more definitely to Christian work. "He is a fine fellow, is Barrie," Virgo had remarked to his friend. "There's only one thing you won't like. He smokes like a chimney-stack!" During the interview, Alexander referred to the habit of smoking, asking Mr. Barraclough if he would feel able to try and drop it. No further word was said on the subject. But after Mr. Barraclough's visit in Scotland had lengthened out to several weeks, and he had undertaken an increasing responsibility at the piano, Alexander asked him how he was succeeding in getting over the smoking habit. Mr. Barraclough looked up at him with astonishment. "Why, I have never touched tobacco in any form since the day you spoke to me in London, Mr. Alexander!" The young man's natural musical ability was shaping itself for the special work required, but perhaps this indication of a strong character helped Alexander's decision to offer him the position of pianist.

Robert Harkness

The following extract gives another account of Alexander's first evangelistic meeting with Harkness as pianist, this time told in the words of Harkness himself. Note his references to the improvisatory character and "full octaves" of the accompaniment.

From George T. B. Davis, *Twice around the World with Alexander, Prince of Gospel Singers* (New York: Christian Herald, 1907), 47–48.

"Dr. Torrey and Mr. Alexander came to my home town of Bendigo [Australia] in June [1902]. Prior to their coming a committee of the Mission came to me, and asked if I would not help in the meetings by playing the piano a part of the time. I was not interested in evangelistic meetings; indeed, I was rather opposed to them, but the thought struck me, that perhaps my good father and mother would be pleased if I took part in these meetings, and I consented. I hadn't been in the first meeting ten minutes before I found it was going to be decidedly warm, much warmer than I had expected.

"Mr. Alexander announced Hymn No. 7, and I was soon playing a two-line hymn, with an old Southern melody. I was not deeply interested, and played it in an offhand way. In playing through the 'Glory Song,' when I came to the chorus, I closed the book; I had memorized it quickly and improvised an accompaniment to the chorus to try to displease Mr. Alexander; but, instead of displeasing him, he turned around and looked at me and said, 'Keep it up. Keep it up. That is what we want.' So I kept on. The next time we had the chorus I played a full octave accompaniment, thinking he would surely be upset, but he was not there to be upset. At the close of the meeting Dr. Torrey asked me if I was a Christian. I straightened up and said, 'No, I am here to play the piano.' Dr. Torrey left me and went away, to pray for me—I think.["]

15
Roman Catholic Pronouncements on Instrumental Music

THE twentieth century saw the most profound changes in the worship of the Roman Catholic church since the Council of Trent and, in some respects went even beyond that sixteenth-century reform in the extent of the reforms that have been promulgated. Many of these changes have, of course, affected the church's music, especially the changeover from Latin to the vernacular and the more active role assigned to the congregation subsequent to Vatican Council II.

The two most important official documents of the twentieth-century Roman Catholic church that deal with music were the *Motu proprio* of Pope Pius X and the *Sacrosanctum Concilium* from Vatican Council II. Both documents allowed the continued use of musical instruments, but repeated familiar admonitions: make sure that the instruments and the music to be played are suitable to the liturgy they accompany.

Pope Pius X

Without doubt, the most significant Roman Catholic pronouncement on music before Vatican Council II was the *Motu proprio* of Pope Pius X (1835-1914), issued in 1903. Instrumental music was dealt with primarily in Section VI of this document.

Pope Pius X, *Motu proprio*, VI. Translated by C. J. McNaspy in *The Motu Proprio of Church Music of Pope Pius X: A New Translation and Commentary* (Toledo: Gregorian Institute of America, 1950), 12-13.

§ 15. Although music proper to the Church is purely vocal, yet music with organ accompaniment is also allowed. In which particular case, within due bounds and with proper safeguards, other instruments can also be admitted, but never without the special permission of the

Ordinary, according to the prescription of the *Caeremoniale Episcoporum*.

§ 16. As the chant must always have first place, the organ or instruments must simply sustain it and never oppress it.

§ 17. It is not permitted to use long preludes before the chant, or to interrupt it with intermezzo pieces.

§ 18. The sound of the organ in accompaniments, in preludes, in interludes and the like, not only must be conformed to the nature of the instrument, but must share in all the qualities that true sacred music possesses, and which are mentioned above.

§ 19. The use of the pianoforte in church is forbidden, as also of noisy or frivolous instruments, such as snare drums, bass drums, cymbalo, bells and the like.

§ 20. It is strictly forbidden for bands to play in church; and only in some special case, with the consent of the Ordinary, will it be allowed to admit a limited choice of wind instruments, provided the composition and accompaniment to be executed be written in a grave, fitting style, and entirely similar to that proper to the organ.

§ 21. In processions outside the church a band may be permitted by the Ordinary, provided no profane pieces are in any way rendered. It would be desirable in such cases for the band to confine itself to accompanying some spiritual canticle in Latin or the vernacular, performed by singers or pious congregations that take part in the procession.

Vatican Council II

The Second Vatican Council was called by Pope John XXIII (1881-1963) shortly after he was elected to the papacy in 1958. The Council met from 1962 to 1965 and paved the way for substantial changes in the liturgy and other aspects of the church's life. The first document to be promulgated was one on the liturgy itself, which noted with approval the traditional place of the pipe organ, but made room for the use of other "suitable" instruments as well.

Vatican Council II, *Sacrosanctum Concilium* (1963), VI, section 120. Translated in International Commission on English in the Liturgy, *Documents on the Liturgy 1963-1979: Conciliar, Papal, and Curial Texts* (Collegeville, Minn.: Liturgical Press, 1982), 25.

120. In the Latin Church the pipe organ is to be held in high esteem, for it is the traditional musical instrument that adds a wonderful splendor to

the Church's ceremonies and powerfully lifts up the spirit to God and to higher things.

But other instruments also may be admitted for use in divine worship, with the knowledge and consent of the competent territorial authority and in conformity with art. 22, § 2, art. 37, and art. 40. This applies, however, only on condition that the instruments are suitable, or can be made suitable, for sacred use, are in accord with the dignity of the place of worship, and truly contribute to the uplifting of the faithful.

16
The Use of Musical Instruments from the Folk, Rock, and Pop Cultures

FUELED by technological innovations, a burgeoning radio and recording industry, and other factors, popular music forms boomed in the years following World War II. Older types of popular music types such as jazz, folk, and country/western reached more people, while new types such as rock were developed and became spectacularly successful. During the 1960s, some of these popular styles began to be adapted to religious text. At first accepted only tentatively by the church, by the end of the twentieth century, this "Contemporary Christian Music" had become a significant component of the music in many British and American congregations, and the only music used in some churches.

The advent of Contemporary Christian Music naturally involved the introduction of the instruments used to accompany this music. Few of these instruments—guitar, drums, saxophone, and so on.—had previously been commonly used in the church, and their introduction has sometimes been controversial, as the writings in this chapter show.

Chuck Kraft

Chuck Kraft is a regular feature writer for *Worship Leader* magazine. In the article reprinted below, the author sees the preference for organ or guitar not simply as a matter of musical taste, but as a reflection of one's view of God, with the organ symbolizing God's transcendence and the guitar God's immanence.

Chuck Kraft, "Organ/Guitar Preference Reflects View of God," *Worship Leader* 2 (April/May 1993), 7.

"Stop them, stop them, stop them!" The voice was that of one of our oldest church members, now over 90 and able to look back on a lifetime of commitment to Christ and to our church. It was the music she was having a problem with. Somebody had brought guitars and (horrors!) a drum into the sanctuary, and the music was disturbing her. For this older saint, such modern music could not glorify God. It was the majestic, awe-inspiring chords of the organ—along with a large pulpit; antique, "biblical" language; a robed preacher; and stained-glass windows—that stirred her soul. Anything "less" disturbed her and, she was sure, disturbed God, since it robbed Him of the honor and majesty due Him.

A lot of traditional (mostly older) Christians don't like the fact that the younger generation has become so attached to guitars. Oh, guitars can be allowed for secular things, for play, for frivolity. But why does the younger generation insist on bringing guitars into the church? "How far can we let things like this go?" the traditionalists ask. "The organ is the instrument of worship. God certainly can't be pleased over a switch to guitars."

There is a problem to be sure. But the underlying issue is not really the music. Rather, buried far below the level of consciousness, is the fact that their whole view of God is under attack. The organ fits that view nicely. So do a large, high pulpit; stained-glass windows; black-covered Bibles; a preacher in robes reading or praying in archaic language; and a somber choir with soloists who project their voices perfectly but are only partly understandable.

All of these remind one of the awesome, holy, distant, barely approachable God. Worship for those with this view should be a very serious thing. One is in the presence of God, and all frivolity, all movement, all enjoyment, is to be left outside. God is majestic. We are to admire Him, but from a distance. This view of God as distant and unapproachable gets reinforced for older generations and taught to the younger ones constantly through the use of vehicles such as organs, pulpits, language, buildings, and the like.

Don't get me wrong. I love organ music. My problem here is not a music problem. It's a theological problem. The question is, what impression, what meaning concerning God is received when an organ is played? By contrast, what impression and meaning concerning God are received when a guitar is played?

Not that it is wrong to portray the awe-inspiring side of God. Our God is truly awesome and majestic, "high and exalted" (Isaiah 6:1). An organ helps us to see Him that way. But if that's all we see, we've missed the most impressive part of God, the part that Jesus focused on most. Jesus continually emphasized His connection with us by referring to Himself as the Son of Man. In becoming a human, He became one of us, uniting God with humanity for eternity. It is this impressive incarnation part that guitars help us with.

Worshiping with guitars portrays a different concept of God. A guitar is a close, uncomplicated instrument. Unlike the organ—a complicated instrument mastered by only a few—a guitar gives the impression that anyone can learn to play it. Furthermore, the player stands on the same level as the audience, not above it in a loft. And the player moves—and encourages the audience to move as well. Can such an instrument be used to honor God?

Let's look at Scripture. John 1:14 says, "So the word of God became a human being and lived among us" (Phillips). An incredible thing—God chose to live among us, not high above and distant from us! God's ultimate revelation of Himself became touchable—on our same level. Furthermore, He (and the authors of Scripture) used languages notable for their folksiness and intelligibility, not for elegance. We rejoice in the incarnation—God coming close, uniting with humankind forever.

Can you imagine Jesus playing an organ? How about a guitar? God has chosen to come close. It is we who choose to push Him away—with music, with pulpits, with stilted translations of Scripture, with preaching styles. Somehow, worship with guitars seems to bring Him close again. So do praying in ordinary language; pastors who speak personally—and come out from behind their pulpits; songs that are joyful, not overly laden with information, and that are directed to God, not just about Him; and our responding with our whole being—not just our minds—to a God who likes to be where we are.

The Lord is here in our midst! How can we be somber? He's come all the way down to our level! How can we be content with worship that pushes Him away again? It's a time for expressions of joy. How can we keep from moving? Jesus wants to participate with us. There He is with the guitarists. It's the theology of incarnation that transforms worship from somberness to pure joy. Three cheers for guitars (and drums)! There's an important theological truth in the switch from organ to guitar.

Richard J. Schuler

The increasing use of the guitar and piano in the worship services of American churches during the last quarter of the twentieth century has not met with universal approval. The following article, written from a Roman Catholic perspective, probably sums up the feeling of many churchgoers, Protestant and Catholic alike. The basic argument is that there is nothing inherently wrong with the guitar and piano, but that they simply do not qualify as sacred instruments because of their associations and their lack of a body of artistic sacred music. As the author cogently expresses it: "I have no problem with the guitar; it is only what is played on it (in church) that troubles me."

Richard J. Schuler, "Guitars and Pianos," *Sacred Music* 111 (Summer 1984), 3-4.

Some years ago the late Archbishop Leo C. Byrne, who was at that time the chairman of the bishops' committee on the liturgy, asked me what I had against guitars. I replied that I had nothing against guitars, but only with what is being played on them.

Today the presence of guitars, and more recently also the piano, as instruments used in liturgical worship, continues to present a problem for the serious church musician who is anxious to carry out the will of the Church in accord with the reforms of the Second Vatican Council. Can one truly say that the guitar and the piano fulfill the directives given by the Church? Here are the pertinent passages from the instruction, *Musicam sacram*, March 5, 1967:

> The pipe organ is to be held in high esteem, for it is the traditional musical instrument that adds a wonderful splendor to the Church's ceremonies and powerfully lifts up the spirit to God and to higher things.
>
> But other instruments also may be admitted for use in divine worship, with the knowledge and consent of the competent territorial authority. . . This may be done, however, only on condition that the instruments are suitable, or can be made suitable, for sacred use, are in accord with the dignity of the place of worship, and truly contribute to the uplifting of the faithful. (Art. 62)
>
> . . . Instruments that are generally associated and used only with worldly music are to be absolutely barred from liturgical services and religious devotions. All musical instruments accepted for divine worship must be played in such a way as to meet the requirements of a liturgical service and contribute to the beauty of worship and the building up of the faithful. (Art. 63)
>
> It is, of course, imperative that organists and other musicians be accomplished enough to play properly. (Art. 67)

The problem resolves itself into the two basic requirements demanded of all musical endeavor for the Church: it must be sacred and it must be art. The council fathers, the documents following on the council, the Holy Father himself, never cease to repeat those two absolute requisites. We must thus ask if the guitar and the piano are sacred, and can the guitar and the piano be used to produce true art for the Church.

Instruments are not in themselves sacred or profane; nothing is sacred or profane (excepting always the Eucharistic Body of Christ and His mystical Body, the Church). Created things become sacred or profane according to the use to which they are put by the general consensus of the community. It is the connotation that determines if certain art—music, painting, architecture, etc.—is sacred or not. Such a determination is not effected in a short period; but rather over a span of years the community accepts such to be the case. Certain styles of art have come to be thought of as "sacred," *i.e.*, dedicated to divine worship. Other styles are associated with entertainment, dancing, the military, patriotism, death. Most people are offended when a style for one human activity is inserted into another area. We don't want a military band playing in church, and we won't expect to hear Gregorian chant at a dance.

Until now, nearly all music composed for guitar and piano has been written for secular purposes. It is not a question of the artistic value of the compositions. Both instruments have a distinguished repertory, but it consists of secular forms: concertos, sonatas, songs, dances, etc. One cannot find music composed by serious musicians for liturgical forms that use the piano or guitar either as solo or as accompaniment. They have not been "sacred" instruments. Why not? Probably the chief reason is that they were not practical for use in large rooms, since they do not make the volume of sound that is associated with the pipe organ or with orchestra. Whether the electric amplification that is used today will change such a judgment remains to be seen. Whether the future may produce works using the piano and guitar for liturgical music is still to be seen. As of now, their repertory is secular and thus they are considered secular instruments. As I told Archbishop Byrne, I have no problem with the guitar; it is only what is played on it (in church) that troubles me.

So much of what afflicts church music today can be laid at the confusion of sacred and secular. There are those who wish to deny any such distinction, but they are not facing the reality of history nor the facts of human nature. Instead of denying the sacred, it would be better to begin to compose a sacred repertory for these instruments, if they are thought to be so useful and desirable. After all, the pipe organ, which we think of as a sacred instrument, was in its beginnings very much of a secular instrument. Through composition of sacred music for it, it came to be thought of as sacred, a process that stretched over many years.

But more is asked by the Church. Not only must music be sacred for use in the liturgy, it must be art. This applies both to composition and to performance. One readily grants that standards of art vary, and circumstances of place and wealth, education and custom, do make a difference in what qualifies. But, in a word, what is offered to God can only be the *best.* I have the uneasy feeling that too often the guitar or the piano is employed because the competency necessary for organ performance is not at hand. This does not mean that the art of piano or guitar performance is not demanding or of high standard. But it does mean that we are allowing inadequate performances on these instruments since the incompetency is tolerated more easily than it is on the organ. Again, it is the loudness that determines things.

Works played on guitar and piano, even for accompaniment purposes, are not part of the great repertory of those instruments. So often what is done is borrowed in the manner of a ballad, a folksong or some popular tune. As art it fails to qualify; as sacred music it does not pass the test. Pope Paul VI said that such music, good for many other purposes, should not be allowed to enter the temple. A sacred text does not necessarily make a piece worthy of liturgical use; the music accompanying the text must itself be sacred and art, both in composition and in performance.

For the most part, up until now, the guitar and piano have not earned the qualification of sacred instruments.

James R. Hart

A recent development in many churches is the use of a "worship band" or "praise team," which often features the playing of musical instruments that are typically used in contemporary pop music.

From James R. Hart, "The Band in the Praise-and-Worship Tradition," in *Music and the Arts in Christian Worship*, ed. Robert E. Webber. Vol. 4 of *The Complete Library of Christian Worship* (Nashville: Star Song, 1994), Book 1, 426-429. It is interesting to compare this document with the writing by J. S. Bach in chapter 9.

Using Contemporary Instruments and Music

The worship band may be defined as any ensemble of musical instruments with a rhythm section foundation. The rhythm section is comprised of drums, bass, and one or more of the following: piano, guitar, organ and/or synthesizer, and percussion. Other instruments in the worship band may include woodwinds, brass, or strings. (Sample instrumentations will follow.) The repertoire of the band generally consists of contemporary music in the pop, jazz, rock, or Latin idioms. (These are general categories. Other ethnic styles may be prevalent in some churches, particularly in areas with non-Western ethnomusicological influences.) . . .

Establishing Cultural Relevance

With almost every great reform or revival movement in church history there has been an associated musical movement toward cultural relevance. In other words, the music of the common people becomes the worship music of the church. For musicians and theologians as well as lay people, the struggle with this trend has been, and continues to be, balancing cultural relevancy of musical style, instrumentation, and so on, with the attempt to reveal God's transcendence in the worship of the faithful. Both elements of relevancy and transcendence are vital to the Christian worship experience. There must be an openness to culturally relevant musical styles and instrumentations and so on, while making certain those relevant musical elements are sanctified by prayer, sacrament, and the Word of God to God's transcendent nature.

The worship band began to be utilized in the late 1960s as an attempt to make Christian worship relevant to the young and unchurched of that generation. It continues to help fulfill that need cross-denominationally and cross-culturally. When sanctified to the Lord's purposes, the worship band significantly aids a congregation to relate to the more contemporary elements of both the congregation and the societal environment. It can provide some familiarity for those who are unfamiliar or uncomfortable with formalities of traditional or liturgical music, while simultaneously providing those same people the opportunity to enter into the relationship of worshiping God. Or for those who just prefer that musical style, it can provide for them a relevant worship experience. There are a number of musicians who desire to use their talents to lead others in worship but do not fit in instrumentally with more traditional musical offerings. The worship band can provide opportunity for these musicians to offer their talents to the Lord in corporate worship leading.

Instrumental Music in Scripture

. . . The scriptural precedent for worship with instrumental music is clear as well as prevalent. The role of the band in worship should be based on that precedent. The band should accompany and help to lead the musical worship of the church. It should inspire and, at times, accompany the God-breathed prophetic Word as it is presented in the congregation. Instrumentalists should assist in the relief of oppression and lead in times of worshipful celebration. They should help believers to enter fully into God's manifested presence and lead them to reflect on the great attributes of God.

Biases Against Musical Styles

In many churches there exist some biases against certain styles of music due to the aesthetic nature of the music or its association with forms of immorality. Those biases are often aimed particularly at contemporary styles of music most prevalently played by worship bands. While we must be diligent in sanctifying styles of music for the Lord's purposes, we must also deal with the biases that exist in the church against those styles. Instrumental music often has a definite aesthetic value, and, sometimes, detrimental associations. It is the job of the church musician or minister of music to exploit musical aesthetics for the kingdom of God; i.e., use the aesthetic value of music to draw people to a place of encounter with the Lord. He or she must also either avoid music with detrimental associational value or gradually re-educate the congregation to receive it. The ministerial effectiveness of music is dependent upon the pure heart of the ministering musician and the receptivity of the listener.

Instrumentation

The instrumentation of a worship band can vary from a small rhythm section up to a full orchestra with rhythm. . . . Below are listed some sample instrumentations:

A. Rhythm section only:
   1. Piano/Keyboard
   2. Guitar
   3. Bass
   4. Drums
   5. Additional keyboard—e.g., organ or synthesizer
   6. Percussion

B. Rhythm section with horns:
   1. Rhythm
   2. Trumpets—1 or 2
   3. Saxes—1 or 2
   4. Trombones—1
   5. Flute

C. Studio Orchestra
   1. Rhythm
   2. Woodwinds
      a. 4 or 5 players doubling on sax, clarinet, flute, and double reeds
      b. Flute
   3. Brass
      a. 3-4 trumpets
      b. 3-4 trombones (bass trombone doubles on tuba)
      c. 2-3 horns
   4. Strings
      a. 3 (at least) Violin I
      b. 2 (at least) Violin II
      c. 1 (at least) Viola
      d. 1 (at least) Cello
      e. Double bass optional
   5. Harp

The attempt should be made to accommodate as many players as possible while taking into account musical and spiritual standards for personnel and available space and instrumentation. It is possible and quite probable that the band could have more players than needed for a certain instrument. For example, there are often too many guitarists. So the players should be rotated, so long as consistency and quality are not sacrificed. Keeping as many players involved as possible helps to keep interest and excitement up when working with volunteers. It also creates resources for additional groups or backup players when needed.

17
Electronic Instruments in the Church

The twentieth century has been a time of great technological change. Some of these changes have affected the types and functions of musical instruments that are used in the worship of the church. This section deals with three significant technological influences on late-twentieth century American church music: the electronic organ, the taped accompaniment, and the synthesizer.

Erik Routley

The development of electronic tone generation in the twentieth century led to the creation of a new type of church instrument, the electronic organ. Designed primarily for churches that either could not or would not pay the cost and upkeep of a pipe organ, the electronic organ became a fixture in many smaller and medium-sized American churches during the 1950s and 1960s. Erik Routley (1917-1982), the author of the following extract, was an English Congregationalist minister who joined the faculty of Westminster Choir College, Princeton, New Jersey, in 1975. Routley was a prolific author in the field of church music, particularly congregational song. The writing below gives some of his opinions regarding the advantages and disadvantages of the electronic organ.

From Erik Routley, *Church Music and the Christian Faith* (Carol Stream, Ill.: Agape, 1978), 109-111.

This brings us to the electronic instrument, which can be regarded as an alternative to the organ. There are some who wish that electronic keyboard instruments were given a name other than "organ" so that comparisons between these and pipe organs could be more objective. To call them organs suggests that they are usurpers.

The basic proposition must be this: there is no inherent inferiority in the electronic principle of sound production. This is normally overlooked by the defenders of the pipe organ. It is no legitimate accusation to say that the electronic organ produces sound by technological means. So does the pipe organ. So, you must admit, does the violin. All humanly made instruments harness physical principles to specific human uses, and that is technology. The question does not turn on the inalienable property of the pipe organ to be better than the electronic instrument. The question is whether *this* electronic instrument serves the purpose better than *this* pipe organ. Inductive generalizations with moral overtones are invariably pernicious. In order to say "All electronic organs are bad organs" you must prove that there is something inseparable from the nature of electronic sound production which precludes such an instrument from giving an agreeable sound, or as good a sound as a pipe organ. Otherwise there is no difference between the attitude of mind that produces the proposition "All electronic organs are unsatisfactory"—meaning, "I am certain beyond correction that the next one I meet will be unsatisfactory"—and the mind which says "All football players are dumb" or "All publishers are unreliable," which similarly means that this is what you determine to predicate of the next football player or publisher you meet.

That said, I now admit that of almost every electronic organ I have encountered I have said, "*This* one is unsatisfactory." But I have a suspicion that the electronic production of tone is just like all the inventions of the twentieth century (in contrast with inventions of the nineteenth) in that because of the oddly demonic character of our age they have gone wrong and rendered as much disservice as benefit. Some historian will explain this, no doubt. The electronic instrument suffers not only from the inherent difficulty (I refuse yet to say "impossibility") of producing good tone, but also from the environment into which it was born—the pop culture, the greedy society, and cut-rate ethic. Electronic organs can be remarkably cheap, and can feed the lust for pretentiousness which disfigures so much of modern bourgeois society. People give rudimentary instruments of this kind to their children for Christmas. This must be recognized and then dismissed from our consideration, because it is an accident, not a property of this kind of instrument.

There is, of course, no disputing the repulsiveness of the glutinous sounds produced by mass-produced electronic instruments for popular entertainment. The worst excesses of the organs of fifty years ago, against which musicians used to protest with horror, are Schantz and Harrison compared with the deliberately distorted noises we get from behind the bar or within the pop band or, we must add, from the public address systems of famous evangelical crusade meetings. The merest suspicion of this is enough to induce in church people an uneasy feeling that the worst of the secular world is creeping in on them. We add to that the too-easy availability of instruments without full pedalboards, or with an octave of toe-bars, compensated with devices like chimes and vibrators and echo-gadgets, and we certainly have an instrument appropriate to the support of whatever hymns they sing in hell.

But that aside, what are the objective advantages and disadvantages of the electronic organ? Cheapness is normally the most important, actually the most delusive. Churches sometimes install these instruments for the wholly spurious reason that the less money is spent on music the better the church will be. The answer to that nonsense, especially when it is piously claimed that the church gives to missions what it withholds from music, is that music is part of the church's mission. And it is actually true that an electronic instrument designed with the needful care and skill can be quite expensive. Still, there is not much that is healthy in the argument that this way you can get a good deal more for a lot less expense.

Adaptability is a more solid advantage. Churches are often still designed so that there is nowhere to put the organ without either stifling its sound or drowning out the congregation. The allocation of space for ranks of pipes is a greater problem than the setting of speakers.

By far the most solid advantage of the electronic organ is relative portability. This affects the British more than Americans. Far more British congregations than American feel that the days of their present physical sanctuary (which may be old, expensive to maintain, unadaptable to modern worship, and geographically ill-sited) are numbered. There is a *prima facie* case, in such circumstances, when an old pipe organ has become unplayable, for installing an electronic instrument. The presence of a new and excellent pipe organ might present a weighty argument in favor of retaining the old premises, whereas the electronic can be moved with little more difficulty than a piano plus a hi-fi system.

It is therefore in unstable or pioneer situations that electronic instruments have their most legitimate market. This prompts an uneasy feeling that the installation of magnificent new pipe organs argues an absence of that pilgrim or pioneer mentality which should actually never be totally forgotten by settled Christian congregations. But the question then is whether in one's zeal for pilgrimage one must sacrifice musical taste.

Pauline Hudson

One of the most significant musical innovations for many churches during the last quarter of the twentieth century was the development of pre-recorded accompaniments for vocal soloists, choirs, and, to a lesser degree, congregational singing. These typically took the form of tape recordings and, more recently, compact disks. In some churches, recordings have been played before or after the service in place of the traditional organ prelude or postlude. In the following article, the author points out the positive features of tape-recorded accompaniments, as well as some of the pitfalls involved in their use.

Pauline Hudson, "Can Technology Replace the Church Choir Accompanist?" *Choral Journal* 30 (October 1989), 23-24.

John Philip Sousa lamented the phonograph's invention, predicting that the mechanical device would one day take over and put musicians out of work.[1] His prophesy may soon come true for today's church accompanist. The boom in Christian popular music is producing a large selection of "easy to use" accompaniment tapes.

With the push of a button, a choir director can eliminate the need for a live accompanist—a fiendishly gratifying thought for some directors. Popular Christian song books with corresponding tapes are now available.[2] Often the tapes come with voice (for rehearsal), and without voice (for performance).

Accompaniment tapes are relatively new items, appearing within the last fifteen years, but really booming during the last five. They parallel the growth of popular religious music heard on Christian radio and television stations. Most tapes are clearly "up-beat," some quite theatrical. Styles range from Country Western and Christian Pop to more traditional music.

For a busy choir director with a volunteer choir, the tapes can have a

[1]From "The Menace of Mechanical Music," *Appleton's Magazine*, September, 1906. Reference found in: Paul E. Bierley, *The Works of John Philip Sousa* (3888 Morse Rd., Columbus, Ohio 43219-3014: Integrity Press, 1984) p. 196.

[2]*The Recording Locator*, published by William J. Burns, Resource Publications, Inc., 160 E. Virginia St. #290, San Jose, California 95112 (Name of index will be changed to *Christian Music Directory* next year [1990]) is usually available in Christian book stores. It indexes songs by title and by popular recording artist.

lot of appeal. The singers are frequently familiar with both the words and the accompaniment, so getting ready for Sunday morning is relatively easy. Choir rehearsal is usually fun, rather like a sing-along, and the finished product is often quite good.

Tapes are helpful at other times too. They are great on church trips, for sing-alongs, or just for listening. New congregations that meet in leased or donated office space use taped music out of necessity. Where a good instrument and a trained accompanist are unavailable, taped music fills a need.

Amateur soloists sometimes prefer tapes to piano or organ accompaniment. One of the advantages of using a tape is the elimination of rehearsals. A singer can pop a tape into a "jam box" at will and practice anytime. There is no need to schedule rehearsal time with a busy (and sometimes paid) church accompanist.

Probably the biggest consideration, however, is the familiarity of the popular taped music, which literally propels the singer along. People who want to sing, but who cannot read music, find that tapes make performance possible for them.

For convenience, for financial reasons, and because of current preference, the church pianist (if not organist) may be going the way of linen tablecloths, homemade bread, and even finger bowls. Will John Philip Sousa's prediction come true?

For anyone really serious about music, there is no question about the value of a qualified accompanist. In the first place, an accompanist does just what the name implies—he or she goes *with* the conductor and the singers in much the same way that a good dancer goes with her partner on the dance floor—accommodating every tempo and mood change. An accompanist is, above all, flexible during practice and performance.

With an accompaniment tape, a choir director is not *really* a conductor, but a kind of intermediary between the *real* conductor (of the taped music) and the choir. Both director and singers must conform to the tape or risk loss of good ensemble. A live accompanist, on the other hand, allows the choir director to shape the music. There is a constant give and take, and a continuous spinning out of the musical work—like the growth of something living.

An amateur soloist especially benefits by having a good accompanist. Most professional pianists and organists can give good advice about dynamics, rhythm, tempo, and sometimes diction. Accompanists aid a singer's musical growth. Also, if problems arise during performance, an accompanist can often cover for the singer. In addition, there is a sense of craftsmanship and artistic integrity when a soloist and accompanist perform well together.

Sometimes a choir director or soloist decides to use a tape in order to get a *big* sound or to imitate a popular rendition. However, if the stereo system is inadequate for the room, the taped accompaniment will be also. It is a sad fact that many performances using tapes are ruined by the intrusion of unmusical sounds and shallow, inadequate accompaniment. Awkward starts and mechanical failures are also problems.

Good four part singing disintegrates (if it is even achieved) by reliance on inadequate accompaniment. During rehearsal, a pianist or organist usually plays the various pitches for the voice parts. Sometimes the accompanist plays the different vocal lines, and even all of the lines together. If the accompanist later performs with the choir, the singers usually maintain their pitches, and good harmony results. Substitution of a tape—with different instrumental timbres and different pitches—can confuse the singers.

The question arises whether accompanists can be replaced. The same point arose decades ago regarding the replacement of teachers by televised instruction. How many congregations would seriously consider replacing their preacher with a taped sermon—regardless of how inspiring the tape or how weak the preacher?

Teachers and ministers create a special group rapport that is essential to their work. Musicians also depend upon human interaction—between themselves, and with the audience. Isn't the artistic unity that arises from a totally live performance a goal worth persuing [sic]?

Church music is rapidly changing. There is now a whole world of popular religious music in addition to traditional hymns and classical works. In many churches the new popular works form a large part of the choral and solo repertoire.

Fortunately, in most cases, good, playable accompaniments are now available. However, accompaniment tapes are a tempting alternative. It is important for church choir directors and accompanists to be aware of the new trend, to assess the musical options, and to ask themselves, "Can technology replace the church choir accompanist?"

James R. Hart

Another significant innovation that has impacted many late twentieth-century American churches has been the development of the synthesizer. Churches have used this instrument in a variety of ways, some of which are detailed in the following article.

James R. Hart, "The Synthesizer in Worship," in *Music and the Arts in Christian Worship*, ed. Robert E. Webber. Vol. 4 of *The Complete Library of Christian Worship* (Nashville: Star Song, 1994), Book 1, 414-415.

The Synthesizer's Impact on Worship

The development and utilization of the synthesizer as a musical instrument has had a revolutionary impact on the music community worldwide. The electronic music industry as a whole, integrating technologies involving computers, synthesizers, software, and advanced networking and communication interfaces, has left an indelible and immensely significant impression on the historical record of musical development. The full impact of this electronic music revolution is yet to be determined but is sure to be monumental.

Let us begin with some definitions. For our purposes, a synthesizer is a musical instrument which produces sound through the physical (analog) or computer-induced (digital) manipulation of electrical current. The parameters of the nature and extent of the electronic manipulation must be programmable by the operator of the instrument (or the musician operating the instrument). So, these two factors are necessary for an instrument or electronic hardware implement to be considered a synthesizer: electronic tone production and human programmability.

The Synthesizer in Worship

How does this development of electronic music technology apply to worship in the church? Biblically and historically, God's people have sanctified and incorporated contemporary technologies into the life of the community of faith. King David sanctified and utilized instruments that were in common usage in other cultures and invented some new instruments in addition. Throughout church history, developments in musical instrument technology have been sanctified (sometimes reluctantly) and used in Christian worship. For example, the pipe organ, now one of the most commonly found instruments in Christian churches, was developed by Egyptians and Greeks for secular usages. The electric guitar, bass, and drums, which, along with the piano, comprise the contemporary rhythm section, have come into common usage in worship after achieving success in the jazz and rock idioms (although many churches still consider the rhythm section to be anathema). To ignore the development of musical synthesis and its potential use in worship would be tantamount to our predecessors in church worship direction ignoring the development of the pipe organ.

The Synthesizer in Place of Acoustic Instruments. The synthesizer is utilized in two often overlapping ways in contemporary worship settings. First, the synthesizer is used to imitate or replace acoustic instruments. Since the extent of its tone production capabilities are so vast, the synthesizer can effectively imitate strings, woodwinds, brass, percussion, or other keyboard instruments (even ancient keyboard instruments). It can fill in the gaps in typical church orchestra settings where instrument groups are often missing. In churches where budgetary restrictions disallow the purchase of an organ or a good piano, the synthesizer can be a feasible, affordable substitute.

However, this application of the synthesizer as an imitating or replacing instrument is limited by the very nature of the instrument. Digital reproduction of sound can never exactly imitate real sound, although it can come very close. The playing of an acoustic instrument is characterized by an investment of a human factor which is not comprehensively reproducible electronically. Also, the sound produced by the synthesizer must be run through a sound system, which tends to further limit its range of harmonic richness. In spite of these limitations, the synthesizer can be effective in filling in instrumental gaps or replacing a piano or organ.

The Synthesizer as a Unique Instrument. The second and possibly more definitive use for the synthesizer is as a unique and distinct musical instrument. It can produce a multitude of sounds and effects that no other instrument is capable of producing. This distinctive character of the synthesizer not only makes for it an irrefutable place in the history of musical instruments, but also provides for it a contemporary application as a member of the rhythm section of an orchestra.

Along with the use of sequencers and other electronic gear, the synthesizer makes such areas as recording and orchestrating much more accessible to the average church musician. As equipment becomes more sophisticated as well as more reasonable in cost, the God-given creative potential in musicians can be nurtured and released, resulting in new ways to communicate and express praise and worship to the Lord.

Further Reading

THE purpose of the following bibliography is to direct the attention of students and other readers to additional sources on the persons and topics covered in this book. The list is necessarily selective and concentrates mainly on writings in English that are likely to be available in college, university, and seminary libraries.

General

Faulkner, Quentin. *Wiser Than Despair: The Evolution of Ideas in the Relationship of Music and the Christian Church*. Westport, Conn.: Greenwood, 1996.

Fox, Lilla M. *Instruments of Religion and Folklore*. New York: Roy Publishers, 1969.

Novotny, Robert J. "Instrumental Music and the Liturgy." *Caecilia* 89 (Summer 1962), 52-70.

Ode, James A. *Brass Instruments in Church Services*. Minneapolis: Augsburg, 1970.

Trobian, Helen R. *The Instrumental Ensemble in the Church*. New York and Nashville: Abingdon, 1963.

Winternitz, Emanuel. *Musical Instruments and Their Symbolism in Western Art*. New York: W. W. Norton, 1967.

The Bible

Aland, Kurt, Matthew Black, Carlo M. Martini, Bruce M. Metzger, and Allen Wikgren, eds. *The Greek New Testament*. 2nd ed. Stuttgart: Württemberg Bible Society, 1968.

Finesinger, Sol Baruch. "Musical Instruments in OT." *Hebrew Union College Annual* 3 (1926), 21-76.

Harris, William. "Echoing Bronze." *Journal of the Acoustical Society of America* 70 (October 1981), 1184-1185.

Sendrey, Alfred. *Music in Ancient Israel.* New York: Philosophical Library, 1969.

Stainer, John. *The Music of the Bible.* Rev. ed. London: Novello, 1914.

Werner, Eric. "'If I Speak in the Tongues of Men . . .' St. Paul's Attitude to Music." *Journal of the American Musicological Society* 13 (1960), 18-23.

The Postbiblical and Medieval Eras

Apel, Willi. *The History of Keyboard Music to 1700.* Trans. and rev. by Hans Tischler. Bloomington: Indiana University Press, 1972.

Bedbrook, Gerald Stares. *Keyboard Music from the Middle Ages to the Beginnings of the Baroque.* London: Macmillan, 1949.

Bowles, Edmund A. "Were Musical Instruments Used in the Liturgical Service during the Middle Ages?" *Galpin Society Journal* 10 (May 1957), 40-56.

Butts, Thomas E. "The Use of Instruments in the Church and Liturgical Events of the Middle Ages." *American Recorder* 13 (February 1972), 6-9.

Caldwell, John. "The Organ in the Medieval Latin Liturgy, 800-1500." *Proceedings of the Royal Musical Association* 93 (1966/67), 11-24.

Hopkins, Edward J. *The English Medieval Church Organ.* Exeter, England: William Pollard, 1888.

McKinnon, James W. "Fifteenth-Century Northern Book Painting and the *a cappella* Question: An Essay in Iconographic Method." In *Studies in the Performance of Late Medieval Music*, ed. Stanley Boorman. Cambridge, England: Cambridge University Press, 1983, pp. 1-17.

———. "The Meaning of the Patristic Polemic against Musical Instruments." *Current Musicology* 1 (Spring 1965), 69-82.

———. *Music in Early Christian Literature.* Cambridge, England: Cambridge University Press, 1987.

———. "Musical Instruments in Medieval Psalm Commentaries and Psalters." *Journal of the American Musicological Society* 21 (Spring 1968), 3-20.

———. "Representations of the Mass in Medieval and Renaissance Art." *Journal of the American Musicological Society* 31 (Spring 1978), 21-53.

Perrot, Jean. *The Organ from Its Invention in the Hellenistic Period to the End of the Thirteenth Century*. Trans. by Norma Deane. London: Oxford University Press, 1971.

Pestell, Richard. "Medieval Art and the Performance of Medieval Music." *Early Music* 15 (February 1987), 57-68.

Williams, Peter. *The King of Instruments: How Churches Came To Have Organs*. London: SPCK, 1993.

———. *A New History of the Organ from the Greeks to the Present Day*. Bloomington and London: Indiana University Press, 1980.

———. *The Organ in Western Culture 750-1250*. Cambridge, England: Cambridge University Press, 1993.

The Sixteenth and Seventeenth Centuries

Arnold, Denis. "Brass Instruments in Italian Church Music of the Sixteenth and Early Seventeenth Centuries." *Brass Quarterly* I (December 1957), 81-92.

———. "Instruments in Church: Some Facts and Figures." *Monthly Musical Record* 85 (February 1955), 32-38.

Bonta, Stephen. "The Use of Instruments in Sacred Music in Italy 1560-1700." *Early Music* 18 (November 1990), 519-535.

Bruinsma, H. A. "The Organ Controversy in the Netherlands Reformation to 1640." *Journal of the American Musicological Society* 7 (1954), 205-212.

Clark, J. Bunker. "The A Cappella Myth!" *American Organist* 47 (April 1964), 16-21.

Dixon, Graham. "Roman Church Music: The Place of Instruments after 1600." *Galpin Society Journal* 34 (March 1981), 51-61.

Fellerer, K. G. "Church Music and the Council of Trent." Trans. by Moses Hadas. *Musical Quarterly* 39 (October 1953), 576-594.

Gotsch, Herbert. "The Organ in the Lutheran Service of the 16th Century." *Church Music* 67, no. 1 (1967), 7-[12].

Klenz, William. *Giovanni Maria Bononcini of Modena: A Chapter in Baroque Instrumental Music*. Durham: Duke University Press, 1962. See especially chapter 11.

Korrick, Leslie. "Instrumental Music in the Early 16th-Century Mass: New Evidence." *Early Music* 18 (August 1990), 359-370.

Kreitner, Kenneth. "Minstrels in Spanish Churches, 1400-1600." *Early Music* 20 (November 1992), 533-546.

Nelson, Bernadette. "Alternatim Practice in 17th-Century Spain: The

Integration of Organ Versets and Plainchant in Psalms and Canticles." *Early Music* 22 (May 1994), 239-256.

Parrott, Andrew. "Grett and Solompne Singing: Instruments in English Church Music before the Civil War." *Early Music* 6 (April 1978), 182-187.

Samuel, Harold E. "Michael Praetorius on Concertato Style." In *Cantors at the Crossroads: Essays on Church Music in Honor of Walter E. Buszin*, ed. Johannes Reidel. St. Louis: Concordia, 1967, pp. 95-109.

Schnoebelen, Anne. "The Role of the Violin in the Resurgence of the Mass in the 17th Century." *Early Music* 18 (November 1990), 537-542.

Selfridge-Field, Eleanor. "Bassano and the Orchestra of St. Mark's." *Early Music* 4 (April 1976), 152-158.

Van Wye, Benjamin. "Ritual Use of the Organ in France." *Journal of the American Musicological Society* 33 (Summer 1980), 287-325.

The Eighteenth and Nineteenth Centuries

Byrne, Maurice. "The Church Band at Swalcliffe." *Galpin Society Journal* 17 (February 1964), 89-98.

Choate, J. E., and William Woodson. *Sounding Brass and Clanging Cymbals: The History and Significance of Instrumental Music in the Restoration Movement (1827-1968).* Henderson, Tenn.: Freed-Hardeman University, 1990.

Eisen, Cliff. "Mozart's Salzburg Orchestras." *Early Music* 20 (February 1992), 89-103.

Kroeger, Karl. "The Church-Gallery Orchestra in New England." *American Music Research Center Journal* 4 (1994), 23-30.

Macdermott, K. H. *The Old Church Gallery Minstrels: An Account of the Church Bands and Singers in England from about 1660 to 1860.* London: S.P.C.K., 1948.

Music, David. "The Introduction of Musical Instruments into Baptist Churches in America." *Quarterly Review* 40 (October 1979), 55-62.

Ochse, Orpha. *The History of the Organ in the United States.* Bloomington and London: Indiana University Press, 1975.

Owen, Barbara. *The Organ in New England.* Raleigh: Sunbury, 1979.

Schulze, Hans-Joachim. "Johann Sebastian Bach's Orchestra: Some Unanswered Questions." *Early Music* 17 (February 1989), 3-15.

Sharp, H. B. "Church Band, Dumb Organist, and Organ." *Galpin Society Journal* 14 (March 1961), 37-40.

Sonneck, O. G. *Francis Hopkinson, the First American Poet-Composer (1737-1791), and James Lyon, Patriot, Preacher, Psalmodist (1735-1794): Two Studies in Early American Music*. Washington, D.C.: H. L. McQueen, 1905.

Temperley, Nicholas. *The Music of the English Parish Church*. 2 vols. Cambridge, England: Cambridge University Press, 1979.

Terry, Charles Sanford. *Bach's Orchestra*. London: Oxford University Press, 1932.

Woods, R. G. "Church Bands and Thomas Hardy." *Early Music* 10 (January 1982), 67-69.

The Twentieth Century

Gentry, Theodore L. "The Origins of Evangelical Pianism." *American Music* 11 (Spring 1993), 90-111.

Hayburn, Robert F. *Papal Legislation on Sacred Music 95 A.D. to 1977 A.D.* Collegeville, Minn.: Liturgical Press, 1979.

Steeves, Cynthia Dawn. "The Origin of Gospel Piano: People, Events, and Circumstances That Contributed to the Development of the Style; and Documentation of Graduate Piano Recitals." D.M.A. dissertation, University of Washington, 1987.

Index

About the Author

David W. Music is Professor of Church Music at Southwestern Baptist Theological Seminary, Fort Worth, Texas. He compiled *Hymnology: A Collection of Source Readings* (Scarecrow, 1996), edited *Oliver Holden (1765-1844): Selected Works* (1998), and coauthored *Singing Baptists: Studies in Baptist Hymnody in America* (1994) with Harry Eskew and Paul A. Richardson. He also served as Editor of *The Hymn*, the quarterly journal of The Hymn Society in the United States and Canada, from 1991 through 1996.